Introduction to commercial law

A comprehensive insight into commercial law careers, including the recruitment process, different types of firms, typical training contract challenges, the skills trainees need to demonstrate, the core practice areas, and common trainee tasks.

successful applications

...riting successful CVs, cover letters and applications,
...wering career and firm motivation questions,
...and strengths from a broad range of

Law firm research, profiles and interview insights

A comprehensive guide to researching law firms, identifying USPs and linking these back to yourself, complete with dozens of firm profiles, detailed assessment centre insights, and example (verified) successful applications and cover letters.

Prepa... ...rviews and assessme... ...res

Practical advice and insider tips on how to effectively tackle assessment centres, including ice breakers, competency and motivation interviews, group and negotiation exercises, presentations, psychometric tests and virtual interviews.

Tackling psychometric tests

An in-depth look at Watson Glaser, verbal reasoning, logical reasoning, situational judgement and numerical tests, including practice test questions and practical tips on how to improve your technique.

Succeeding during internships

Guidance on how to convert internships into job offers, including insights into how firms expect you to behave, how to tackle the work, how to excel during team presentations and negotiation exercises, and how to prepare for final interviews.

Commercial awareness in context

This course explains the meaning of commercial awareness, how it comes up in interviews, how to develop it, what to consider when discussing current affairs, and how to structure your answers to commercial awareness questions.

Mergers and acquisitions

This course offers a solid grounding in the legal, commercial and financial knowledge required for commercial law interviews and internships, including explanations of key M&A-related terminology and jargon.

Discussing current affairs and industry trends

This course offers in-depth advice on how to research into and confidently discuss current affairs. It also covers key current affairs from throughout 2020 and 2021, and provides insights into legal industry trends and legal technology.

Interview case studies

This course talks you through two case studies from real commercial law interviews, including discussion of the role of the firm's key practice areas and various legal and commercial terms and concepts.

The business of law firms

An insider insight from an ex-City partner into how law firms operate as businesses, including firms' operating models, client fee structures, financial metrics, key stakeholders, business development initiatives, expansion strategies, and more.

Legal technology

An insider insight into key challenges faced by law firms and in-house teams, how firms use legal tech to combat these challenges, cutting-edge legal tech products, and how document automation actually works in practice (including a real life demo).

Practical networking and LinkedIn

An in-depth guide to networking, including practical tips for networking one-on-one and in a virtual setting, advice on how to use LinkedIn effectively, and personal insights and anecdotes to help you boost your confidence and shift your mindset.

Delivering effective presentations and managing nerves

Expert guidance on delivering effective presentations, including tips on how to communicate with confidence, manage nerves, prepare effectively, engage listeners, use visual aids appropriately, and present in a team.

Join our LinkedIn community

This group was set up to enable candidates pursuing a career in commercial law to access and share tips, insights and resources relating to commercial law applications, interviews and internships.

We regularly share our own knowledge and experience, as well as tips around employability and commercial awareness, key legal and commercial definitions, links to other great resources and opportunities, early previews of new books and exclusive discounts.

Join the exclusive City Career Series Commercial Law Applicants group on LinkedIn via:

www.linkedin.com/groups/8944518

Training Contract Handbook

With expert contributions from dozens of trainees and associates from a range of market-leading City firms, plus comprehensive insights and insider tips from leading City trainers, authors and academics, this unique training contract survival guide offers:

- Explanations of hundreds of key legal concepts and contractual clauses, including the terminology, jargon and acronyms that you'll likely come across in practice.
- A comprehensive insight into what trainees do, including practice area overviews, example trainee work-logs and a summary of the challenges trainees face.
- Insider tips on managing your workload, interacting with supervisors, taking instructions, demonstrating initiative, building a personal brand, networking and negotiating.
- Expert guidance on how to effectively approach legal and business research, presentations, proofreading and written tasks.
- A summary of foundational commercial and contract law principles, including contract formation, the allocation of risk, limitations of liability, restrictive covenants, boilerplate clauses, security and insolvency.
- Advice on how to project manage the M&A process, including an insight into auctions and bilateral sales, the role of key legal practice areas, and signings and completions.
- A comprehensive insight into complex due diligence exercises, including an overview of the role of trainees and the key issues to look out for.
- A detailed explanation of key transaction documents, including engagement letters, non-disclosure agreements, sale and purchase agreements, shareholders' agreements and loan agreements.
- An insight into the work carried out by dispute resolution teams and an overview of key methods of dispute resolution.
- Explanations of key litigation documents and processes, including advice on how to co-ordinate large-scale document reviews.
- A practical guide to Microsoft Word, Microsoft Outlook and Microsoft Excel.

Legal Practice Course Handbook

Written only by authors that were awarded distinctions on the LPC before embarking on training contracts with top City firms, the LPC Handbook is a Legal Practice Course revision guide that covers the following core modules:

- Business Law, Accounts & Taxation
- Property Law
- Civil Litigation
- Criminal Litigation
- Professional Conduct & Regulation
- Wills & Administration of Estates
- Solicitors' Accounts
- Drafting & Skills

Detail and coverage

This is the most detailed LPC revision guide available. It includes: a multitude of defined terms; comprehensive, yet easily digestible explanations of key concepts; a variety of procedure plans and flowcharts; and full statutory references throughout.

Presentation and format

This is the only full colour LPC revision guide on the market, which ensures that concepts can be introduced and explained as clearly and concisely as possible. The format has been developed over a number of years to facilitate readers' understanding and retention of information.

Illustrative examples

There are many practical, illustrative examples of exam questions and suggested answers throughout this guide, helping to clarify and contextualise the information contained in each topic.

Other City Career Series Publications

City Career Series offers a comprehensive range of resources directly relevant to the recruitment process for a wide variety of City careers. We have published a series of additional guides that offer a solid grounding in the general knowledge required for City interviews and internships (see below).

Commercial Law Handbook

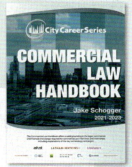

The Commercial Law Handbook offers a solid grounding in the legal, commercial and financial knowledge required for commercial law interviews and internships, including explanations of the key terminology and jargon. This includes detailed advice and insights covering:

- Commercial awareness and case study interviews, assessment centres more generally, and how to gain insights into the legal profession.
- What "commercial awareness" means, why it is relevant, how it might be assessed and how to build it.
- How to structure your responses when discussing current affairs and tackling case study questions.
- The role of commercial lawyers, trainee solicitors more specifically, and the main commercial law practice areas.
- Core commercial law principles, including explanations of how contracts are formed, how contractual terms can be used to allocate risk and how security can operate to protect lenders and facilitate corporate borrowing.
- Strategic challenges and commercial considerations relating to starting, running and growing a business.
- Different methods of financing and selling businesses, including the benefits and drawbacks of loans, bonds and IPOs.
- The M&A process, complete with an overview of the key parties that are typically involved and the various issues that can arise.
- Basic economics concepts and financial accounting principles, plus an introduction to Microsoft Excel.
- Key transactional documents and contractual clauses commonly used by commercial lawyers.
- How to convert internships into full-time jobs.

Investment Banking Handbook

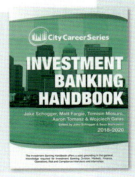

The Investment Banking Handbook offers a solid grounding in the general knowledge required for Investment Banking Division, Markets, Finance, Operations, Risk and Compliance interviews and internships. The handbook includes:

- A description of the role of different banking divisions.
- Consideration of issues relating to starting, running and growing a business.
- Analysis of different methods of purchasing and selling businesses.
- A breakdown of the benefits and drawbacks of various types of financing.
- Descriptions of different business valuation techniques and methods.
- An introduction to basic economics concepts and financial accounting.
- An insight into the M&A process, complete with an overview of key parties that are typically involved.
- Descriptions of the processes that facilitate transactions involving debt and equity finance.
- Focused sections on the Investment Banking and Markets divisions.
- Definitions of key commercial terms.
- An overview of key Microsoft Excel formulas and shortcuts.
- Explanations of how to tackle market sizing questions and brainteasers.
- General interview advice relating to competency, commercial awareness and case study interviews and guidance on how to convert internships into full-time jobs.
- A recommended reading list.

Consultancy Handbook

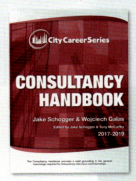

The Consultancy Handbook offers a solid grounding in the general knowledge required for consultancy interviews and internships. The handbook includes:

- An overview of the role of consultants, the various types of consultancy firms and the industries typically serviced by consultants.
- An insight into the recruitment process, with particular focus on how to prepare for and tackle case study interviews.
- An explanation of issues relating to profitability and how to apply the Profitability Framework in case study interviews.
- An insight into the strategic and operational challenges that businesses can encounter and the way in which the Business Situation Framework can be used to tackle related case interview questions.
- An introduction to mergers and acquisitions, including the potential benefits for companies.
- An overview of market sizing questions and brainteasers, complete with examples of how to solve them.
- Examples of other case study analysis tools including the SWOT, Porter's Five Forces and PESTLE frameworks.
- An introduction to key accounting, finance, business valuation and economics concepts.
- An overview of key Microsoft Excel formulas and shortcuts.
- Definitions of key commercial terms.
- General interview advice relating to competency, commercial awareness and case study interviews and guidance on how to convert internships into full-time jobs.

Business Writing Handbook

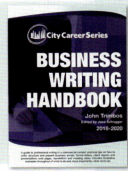

John Trimbos has decades of experience delivering interactive, practical and engaging courses that have helped tens of thousands of professionals to develop essential business skills. The Business Writing Handbook is the product of his experience, providing a comprehensive guide to professional writing in a commercial context. The handbook includes:

- Comprehensive guidance on how to write, structure and present business emails, formal letters, client reports, and presentations, web pages, newsletters and meeting notes.
- Detailed model examples of the above forms of business correspondence, including illustrations of what not to do.
- Advice on how to use visuals and aids to readability most effectively.
- An overview of English grammar, spelling and punctuation rules, with a focus on the most common errors made in a business context.
- A strategy for improving your writing style to achieve maximum impact and clarity when liaising with clients and colleagues.
- Practical tips on effective proof reading and editing in different contexts.
- Humorous examples of terrible errors made where people have failed to follow the rules and guidance set out in this handbook.

These handbooks are available from **CityCareerSeries.com/Store** and **amazon**.co.uk

Contents

Introduction

I have had the pleasure of delivering countless presentations over the past few years on the topics covered in this handbook, often alongside a selection of friends and colleagues who have secured internships and jobs across a broad range of industries. I would like to thank all of them for their insights, which have contributed to my thinking and therefore to the content of this handbook.

This handbook offers a comprehensive range of tips, insights and guidance designed to help you successfully negotiate the recruitment process for a wide range of City careers. However, I would like to acknowledge that there is no objectively *correct* way to approach applications, tests, interviews and internships. I have simply collated the key pieces of advice that I would personally have found useful when first embarking upon my career pursuit. On that note, to give an overview of what's to come, this handbook includes detailed advice on:

- Boosting your employability, including how to accumulate key experiences that can demonstrate and facilitate your personal development.

- Networking confidently and effectively, including an explanation of why networking is important.

- Identifying your priorities and distinguishing between different graduate opportunities.

- Successfully approaching CVs, cover letters and LinkedIn profiles.

- Structuring application answers and preparing effectively for assessment centres.

- Tackling the most commonly asked competency, strengths-based and ethical questions, including illustrative examples of how to draw skills and strengths from your experiences.

- Articulating your career and firm motivations and carrying out targeted research to support your answers.

- Building your commercial awareness, including your knowledge and understanding of topical current affairs.

- Approaching psychometric, situational judgement and e-tray tests.

- Converting internships into graduate job offers.

Importantly, I hope this handbook encourages you to reflect on your experiences, skills, strengths, weaknesses and motivations and helps you to understand how to use this reflection to form the basis of authentic, well-structured answers that enable you to truly stand out.

However, you must remember that your application answers, psychometric test scores, interview responses and internship performances are not the only elements that firms assess. Top organisations expect strong academic performances at university, usually from the very beginning (especially law firms), so make sure you study hard in your first year, even if it doesn't count towards your degree classification. Moreover, not all firms approach recruitment identically. Some firms may reject an application if a single spelling mistake is found. Some may focus more on international experience or language abilities. Some may have higher thresholds for psychometric tests or care more about university grades than others. The list goes on...

It's also important that you never lie during interviews and that you are able to substantiate any statements you make. Recruiters are very skilled at noticing if you are trying to bluff your way through, especially if you've been asked to provide a lot of detail when recounting experiences. Getting caught lying or overly embellishing the truth reflects negatively upon your character and is likely to cause recruiters to question the other statements you have made. At the end of the day, they are looking to get to know the *real* you.

A special thank you to Sarah Cockburn, without whose continuous support and advice this handbook may never have materialised. A huge thanks to the City Career Series team (Carly Schogger and Chris Phillips) for their incredible hard work, creativity and enthusiasm. A massive thank you to Claire Leslie for her extensive edits and invaluable suggestions and Hannah Salton and Lucas Pringle for their incredibly helpful contributions. Thanks also to Susan Vollmer for her fantastic work on the City Career Series videos and Anne Wilson for her advice relating to strengths-based questions. Thanks also to Christopher Stoakes for all his advice and support and for providing the inspiration for the City Career Series handbooks. Thanks to all those that have supported me throughout this project, in particular Frida, Hugo, Ella, Donna, Danny and Carly Schogger, Poppy, Tomisin Mosuro, Alice Toop, Kai Majerus, Hugh Beale and the lawyers that I met whilst interning for all their lectures, inspiration, proofreading, comments and suggestions. Thanks to Sean McCaffrey and Philip Dekker for helping me find my way into commercial law and to Jasmine Schembri for involving me in the university society that inspired this handbook. Thank you to Vinay Mistry for designing citycareerseries.com and Chris Phillips (www.cphillipsdesign.uk) – who deserves a second mention – for his endless patience and fantastic graphic design work. Thanks to the members and the executive committee of Warwick Finance Societies for all the positive responses and useful feedback relating to earlier drafts of this handbook over the years.

Boosting Your Employability

This chapter offers a variety of insights into the actions you can take to boost your employability, from learning about careers and firms, securing industry experience, and applying for part-time work, to making the most of your time off, getting involved in academic and commercial activities, taking on positions of responsibility, exploring a range of extracurricular activities, and building your commercial awareness.

Getting started

If you are just starting out on your career path, the sheer number of industries, firms, divisions within firms and opportunities available can be quite overwhelming and confusing! Whatever you do, keep an open mind. You could start by trying to gain an insight into a range of careers and firms. Look at different industries, large firms, small firms, niche firms, corporations with in-house professional services teams and any other options that sound interesting. This will not only broaden your understanding of how the City works, but could also ensure that your future decisions are better informed (it is important to remember that the City is not for everyone). With all this in mind, below is a simplified overview of the types of opportunities generally offered by large City firms for students and graduates.

Opportunities by year of study

First-year students can usually apply for brief insight opportunities at organisations' offices, typically lasting from a few hours to one week. These tend to involve little or no responsibility, but can (depending on the firm) lead to fast-track opportunities. At the very least, you should have the opportunity to learn more about the relevant industry, gain deeper insights into the firm and network with at least a few employees. Plus, sticking these opportunities on your CV can provide evidence of your research and commitment to the career, which can bolster your application for a full internship further down the line.

Penultimate year students can typically apply for longer internships (lasting 2 weeks – 10 weeks), which can involve real work, more responsibility and a range of assessments. Firms tend to differ in their approaches in terms of what they are willing to offer second year students completing 4 year degrees, so if this is you, be sure to carefully check your eligibility for schemes before applying. Some firms also offer internships to finalists and graduates, although other firms prefer finalists and graduates to apply directly for jobs. After graduation, some industries require candidates to continue with further study, either full-time for a limited period (e.g. the Legal Practice Course before a legal training contract), or part-time whilst also working for the firm (e.g. when accountants and actuaries have to take additional professional examinations).

Opportunities across different industries

Investment banking

Investment banks tend to offer Spring Weeks for first-year students completing a three-year degree and second-year students completing a four-year degree. Spring Weeks typically include group exercises, a series of presentations and work shadowing opportunities, but will usually involve little or no "real" work or responsibility. They can however lead to fast-track opportunities, depending on the firm. Full 10-12 week summer internships are then typically available for penultimate and final year students, although some internships also cater to graduates. These internships typically involve candidates in real work (which can mean long working hours!) and may also include a range of assessments throughout.

Commercial law

Commercial law firms tend to offer insight days for first year students, although a select few offer two-day or week-long experiences. Some firms also offer open days for students at any stage in their education (including graduates). Firms tend to differ in their approaches in terms of what they are willing to offer second year students completing four year degrees, so if this is you, be sure to check your eligibility for schemes before applying. These shorter opportunities tend to involve little or no responsibility, but can include work shadowing, group exercises, and presentations from lawyers and graduate recruiters. Depending on the firm, some can also lead to fast-track opportunities. At the very least, you should have the opportunity to learn more about the legal industry and the role of commercial lawyers, gain deeper insights into the firm, and network with at least a few employees.

Many firms then offer longer internships for penultimate year students around the Christmas break, during Easter and/or over the summer. These longer internships typically last for between two and four weeks and can involve real work (interns will also usually have the opportunity to sit in one or two departments during the experience), more responsibility and a range of assessments. Some firms also offer internship opportunities for graduates, although many prefer graduates to apply directly for training contracts.

Before being recognised as a qualified solicitor, traditionally you needed to complete the Legal Practice Course (LPC) followed by a period of "recognised professional training" which normally lasts for two years and is generally referred to as a "training contract". Non-law students also had to complete the Graduate Diploma in Law (GDL) law conversion course before embarking upon the LPC. However, this is now changing. Whilst many large firms currently still require you to take the LPC (and GDL for non-law students), the Solicitors Regulation Authority (SRA) has now launched the "Solicitors Qualifying Examination" route to qualification, and will eventually phase out the GDL and LPC. The SQE route involves a series of centralised examinations and skills assessments, which will enable individuals to qualify as lawyers without needing to first complete a typical academic law degree or conversion course, as well as the LPC. As part of the SQE qualification, all candidates will also need to complete the equivalent of at least two years of full-time qualifying work experience.

Consultancy, accountancy and other financial services firms

Consultancy, accountancy and other financial services firms differ more in their approach. Some offer insight days/weeks catering for first year students (for instance the PWC Talent Academy, the Accenture Boot Camp, the McKinsey Discover programme and the EY Leadership Academies), although longer internships are still generally reserved for students further along in their studies. As with commercial law and investment banking opportunities, shorter opportunities are likely to involve less responsibility (effectively giving you the opportunity to learn more about the firm and industry), whilst longer internships typically involve you in real work and give the firm the opportunity to assess you more carefully.

Other opportunities

You may also have access to informal insight opportunities offered by university societies. These tend to be less competitive and involve a less onerous application process, yet can still provide you with valuable insights that can inform your future career-decisions (and look great on a CV). Some firms also offer other opportunities that can help you to get a foot in the door, meet employees and potentially access fast-track opportunities for formal internships further down the line. For example, some firms recruit students who have just completed their first year to become campus ambassadors (a role for which you may get paid).

Many firms are also committed to increasing diversity, so if you are from an underrepresented background or have a disability, there may be specific opportunities open to you. If you are at university, you can learn a lot about industries, firms and the opportunities available by attending firm presentations and speaking to your university career service. You can also gain valuable insights from websites such as CommercialLaw.Academy, brightnetwork.co.uk and the websites of the firms to which you are considering applying.

Building a broad base of experience

Firms want to recruit well-rounded individuals who have clearly developed relevant foundational skills. When assessing these skills, firms will look at your range of experiences and achievements in professional, academic and non-academic contexts, including your academic results, work experience (including employments, casual jobs, and relevant placements), positions of responsibility (both academic and non-academic), and extra-curricular activities and interests (including volunteering).

If you only have academic experiences to demonstrate your competencies, this may not present you as a well-rounded individual and could suggest that you wouldn't necessarily fit with the firm's culture or interact well with the firm's employees. In contrast, if you have only non-academic extracurricular experiences to draw from, a firm may doubt whether you have developed the ability to perform and interact with others in a professional context. On that note, I was rejected from my very first interview because the interviewer felt that I had not accumulated a sufficiently broad range of experiences. They reached this conclusion on the basis that I hadn't used any academic or professional examples to demonstrate my skills during the competency interview.

With this in mind, try to accumulate a broad range of experiences, including taking up positions of responsibility and getting involved in university societies and university (or local) clubs and initiatives. Doing so will provide the opportunity to develop your knowledge, skills and confidence (which you can then draw upon on application forms and during interviews), plus you'll probably have a far richer university experience as a result. Ultimately, you should constantly be asking yourself whether your university is in any way *different* because you were there, and whether *your* contributions enhanced other students' experiences.

As well as pursuing your passions and hobbies, you should also try to dedicate some of your free time to developing your commercial awareness. Remember, your commercial awareness is tied to your employability, so you should see boosting your commercial awareness as another key aspect of boosting your employability.

Work experience

If you have undertaken work experience – regardless of whether it is paid or unpaid, or as an intern in a professional services firm or as an office or shop assistant – this will boost your employability. Through such experiences, you'll likely be able to demonstrate a strong work ethic and an ability to commit to an organisation. Depending on your role, you may also be able to demonstrate that you have accumulated at least some experience interacting with clients, working in a team with colleagues, adhering to deadlines, and balancing multiple responsibilities.

Have you worked in the family business? Have you worked in customer services, perhaps as a checkout assistant or a bartender? Have you already visited firms in the industry to which you are applying (even if only for a few hours or for an informal office visit)? I listed working in a small office, working in the music industry, completing a paper round and working at Waitrose (pushing trolleys) as examples of my previous work experience, alongside more relevant industry experience (such as firm office visits). Many firms felt that these examples demonstrated a strong work ethic and that my decision to embark upon a highly pressurised career was better informed as a result of the comparison that such work experiences provided.

To give another example, if you have tutored younger students (be it maths, music, English or dance), this will likely have required you to interact professionally with them (and perhaps their parents), keep them motivated and engaged, communicate complex concepts in an easily digestible manner, organise and plan your lessons, adhere to deadlines, and adapt your approach to support tutees with differing abilities, of different ages, from different backgrounds and cultures, and so on. Doing all this will most likely have honed your organisational, communication, interpersonal and client-facing skills, your confidence, and so on. Perhaps a broader range of skills than you could develop whilst simply work shadowing in an office, or working on academic assignments. Note that there are many tutoring opportunities out there, with companies such as MyTutor connecting freelance tutors with clients (note that freelancing in and of itself can demonstrate independence, commercial awareness, and various other skills).

That aside, try to gain an insight into a range of different careers. Exploring industries and organisations should broaden your understanding of how the City works, whilst also ensuring your personal decisions and career choices are better informed. Keep an open mind, as you may well have preconceptions about certain industries that do not reflect the reality of working within them. I have many friends who started out thinking that they wanted to work in one industry only to decide (having gained experience in a variety of different organisations) that they in fact wanted to work in quite another. Others have decided that they would be happier working for small, niche, or regional firms instead of large City firms, or for a department within a corporation.

You could reach out directly to firms to ask for work experience. Cold calling and emailing *can* work, although you may have more luck with smaller firms (which typically lack the budget to promote and run structured internships, whereas larger firms tend to stick more to their formal schedules of opportunities). It might be best to start by utilising any contacts you may have. Family, friends and friends of family may be able to help out, as may university lecturers, tutors and careers advisers. You could also join various interest groups (e.g. Facebook or LinkedIn groups for start-ups and local businesses) and ask whether there are any work experience opportunities available.

Making the most of university holidays

If you have not secured an internship, or have an internship that takes up only a proportion of a university holiday, start thinking about how best to use any free time you may have. Many firms in interviews will ask how you have spent your 3 – 4 month summer break and "watching Netflix" is never a great answer. Use your time off to do something interesting – something that sets you apart from other candidates – as this will provide firms with an insight into your character. For example, are you the kind of person who uses your initiative and drive to actively pursue your passions and interests? Do you have a desire to experience different cultures? Are you committed to nurturing your personal growth and development? Do you push yourself by leaving your comfort zone from time to time?. If you want firms to believe that the answer to these questions is "yes", then make sure you evidence it with the way you spend your free time.

As mentioned above, carrying out professional work experience can be a good use of your time off. However, there are also various summer programmes that can look great on your CV and be a lot of fun (e.g. government-funded study programs or placements at summer camps through agencies such as Camp America), as well as an increasing number of "virtual" insight experiences and mini-internships. Alternatively, there are a broad range of volunteering and charity initiatives available, both domestically and abroad, that could provide unique and interesting experiences whilst also enhancing your employability.

If instead of carrying out formal or informal work placements you decide to spend your summers travelling, you could utilise this experience to present yourself as a motivated individual with an interest in experiencing different cultures. Travel can also provide a really interesting topic of conversation in interviews; on more than one occasion, I spent a large proportion of an interview with a City firm discussing a study programme I had completed in India. It's also important to remember that once you embark upon your career, you will no longer have the opportunity to travel for extended periods of time (without having to work), so make the most of it! Moreover, travelling can help you to develop a wide range of skills, most notably your confidence, ability to adapt to different cultures, interpersonal skills, resilience, and organisation skills (especially if you are travelling around a continent with questionable transport links!). Travelling also shows that you are willing to place yourself outside of your comfort zone.

Alternatively, you could take a summer job, start a project (for instance, found a small business or do something creative), take an online course (for example, a coding, social media marketing or graphic design course), or pursue some other passion (photography, knitting, music, sport etc.). This can reflect positively on your motivation, ambition, entrepreneurial spirit, work ethic and a whole host of other attributes and skills. City Career Series began as an extracurricular project whilst I was at university!

Academic and commercial activities

You could also consider joining and actively participating in academic societies. Your university may well have a Commercial Law, Finance, Debating or Business society that you could join, as well as a society linked to your degree subject. If your membership leads to you attending particularly interesting presentations or participating in skill-enhancing interactive case studies, then you could use these experiences as examples to demonstrate to firms that you put your free time to good use. Participating in the likes of Young Enterprise, Duke of Edinburgh, Model United Nations or interactive business challenges/case studies at school or during your degree could also reflect positively on you, so perhaps sign up for similar initiatives if you feel that your CV is lacking.

Particular modules or group work exercises that you have undertaken whilst studying can also provide interesting talking points during interviews and deliver an insight into how you have developed your knowledge and capabilities. In addition, there is an increasing range of competitions aimed at students, from essay, research and presentation competitions, to business challenges and hackathons. Perhaps enter some of these, especially those run by any firms you intend to apply to. In order to highlight my academic extracurricular activities, my CV included my membership of various commercial societies and my involvement in the Study India and Study China programmes. I also talked about my engagement in team-based business modules at university and participation in firm-led business challenges on campus.

Positions of responsibility

Firms need to know that their employees can effectively take on responsibility and subsequently manage their time effectively to ensure tasks are completed to the standard required and within the deadlines set. Taking up positions of responsibility at university whilst maintaining a strong academic performance can really help to demonstrate this ability. Try to join the executive committees of the university societies and clubs that most interest you. It doesn't matter whether it's the Finance Society, Music Theatre Society, Ice Hockey Club or a charitable society. It doesn't matter whether you're a first year representative, President, Club Captain or Head of Marketing. The premise is the same: these experiences give you scope to prove to firms that you have the ability to handle responsibility and to demonstrate what you are capable of achieving if given the chance. Find out when elections are taking place, as these are usually open to anyone wishing to apply. Getting to know the current executive committee and members of a society – and demonstrating your interest in getting involved – could increase your chances of being elected or appointed. So attend events, offer to help out, and try your hand at networking. If you apply for a range of roles, you're bound to get something!

If at school you were selected as a Prefect, Ambassador or Head Boy/Girl, or you were elected/appointed onto some sort of student liaison or event committee, this counts as a position of responsibility. Mentoring can similarly evidence your ability to handle responsibility, and there are many organisations that promote voluntary mentoring opportunities for undergraduates (for example www.zerogravity.co.uk). Campus or brand ambassador roles would also count, and it's perfectly fine to state these on applications to rival firms; if anything, it validates you as a candidate, as you passed the recruitment process implemented by another firm). On my CV, I listed: drum kit teacher, founder of a (casual) 5-a-side football team, my role as campus ambassador for a City firm and my role as President of the Commercial Law Society (and later, Warwick Finance Societies) among my positions of responsibility. These are just a few examples. All of your experiences may be relevant and show that you are the sort of person who throws yourself into challenges and opportunities. And with a little lateral thinking and open-mindedness, you can derive a surprising number of skills from each (I cover this in more detail later on in this handbook).

Other extracurricular activities

If you have great grades and relevant work experience, why do extra curriculars matter? How can playing netball, learning an instrument, being on a society exec, carrying out charity work, travelling, or tutoring possibly demonstrate your ability to succeed in a professional role? Well, firms ultimately want to recruit well-rounded individuals who have clearly developed the essential foundational skills needed to thrive. And these foundational skills are just as likely – if not more likely – to be developed as a result of your participation in extra-curricular activities.

To that end, in one interview, I was asked whether I should drop some of my extra-curricular activities to increase my chances of securing a 1st class degree. I said no, on the basis that the skills I have developed (and would continue to develop) as a result of my extra curriculars were equally – if not more – valuable than gaining a 1st, and this didn't stop me securing an internship offer (suggesting the interviewer – at least to some extent – agreed!). Saying that, grades are still important (and the degree of importance changes from firm to firm), so it's important that you strike a balance between academics and experience. Plus I genuinely had a unique breadth of extracurricular activities to support my answer; had I only been involved in a couple, my answer might not have gone down so well.

It is easy to get involved in non-academic extracurricular activities, at least on a casual basis and at a non-competitive level. You can even be a complete beginner. I was never good enough to get into the official university football team, but this didn't stop me from setting up a 5-a-side football team. Ultimately, you want to demonstrate that you have a range of interests and the motivation and initiative to pursue them. You want to prove that you're willing to remove yourself from your comfort zone and try something new. I once even attended an American football training session, but the less said about that the better!

Sport

Do you play for the university netball team? Do you play in (or manage) a casual 5-a-side team? Do you enjoy horse riding? Have you run a marathon or climbed a mountain? Do you enjoy diving, skiing or playing table tennis? If so, have you pursued these interests by joining a club? Attending regular training sessions or regularly involving yourself in a particular sport can demonstrate your ability to commit, your determination, your ability to motivate yourself and others, and your time management skills. In addition, don't forget that being on the committee of a sports club counts as a position of responsibility – whether you're captain of the netball team, treasurer of the rugby club, or president of the karate society – and this can demonstrate a broad range of additional skills (we cover this in more detail in the *Competencies, Strengths & Experience* chapter later on). Finally, if you have done something particularly interesting and unique, mention it! I mentioned that I had gone cage diving with great white sharks, which provided an interesting talking point during interviews (although my wife still makes jokes about me doing this).

Music, art, dance and theatre

Do you sing or play an instrument? If so, do you rehearse and perform with your university orchestra or do you sometimes perform at open "mic" nights? Perhaps you like to perform in theatre productions or dance competitions, or act in short films? Alternatively, do you paint, create videos or carry out graphic design work? These types of experiences can demonstrate that you have the creativity sought after by top City firms (which can be helpful when trying to provide innovative solutions to unique client problems). They can also demonstrate that you have developed the confidence, communication skills and team working abilities required to succeed in a client-led industry.

Volunteering and charitable initiatives

Have you raised money for charity, helped at an orphanage, been involved in school or university charitable initiatives or volunteered at music festivals? This could demonstrate your desire to work for a firm that offers volunteering opportunities (for instance, pro bono legal work), whilst also showing that you are an ethical person. It can also provide interesting anecdotes for interviews. I volunteered to work with the Glastonbury Festival Recycling Crew for many years, which effectively involved taking a position as an unpaid bin man. However, it was great fun, I met a broad range of people and I accumulated some great experiences to draw from when answering application and interview questions.

If you talk a lot about volunteering in your application/interview and then secure an internship, look for opportunities to get involved in the firm's volunteering initiatives during that internship. This will help to demonstrate that the statements you made were sincere. I got involved in various charitable initiatives during internships, which certainly helped to substantiate the statements that I had previously made. A note of caution however: avoid suggesting that your decision to apply to a particular City organisation was based primarily upon the volunteering opportunities on offer to its employees. Volunteering opportunities are nice "add-ons" that can help to enhance your job satisfaction, but they are separate from the City firms' core revenue generating activities. City employers want to know that you are keen to help them make money and/or improve performance. After all, these firms are businesses, not charities (no matter how much they may focus on their altruistic side during presentations).

Travel

Have you studied abroad or travelled to interesting places? Have you completed a ski season or been on a university trip abroad? Have you participated in "Jailbreak", a charity initiative which involves attempting to travel as far away from your university as possible in 36 hours, without spending any money (I reached Munich)? If so, remember to explain *why/how* this has made you a more suitable candidate. Such experiences could evidence: your ability to adapt to different cultures, organise yourself effectively and remain positive whilst under pressure; your desire to work in an international setting; and that you are an interesting, open-minded individual.

Commercial awareness

Trying to "cram" commercial awareness right before an interview isn't an ideal approach, as you'll likely only pick up a shallow understanding of the commercial topics that you read about. Get into the habit of building your commercial awareness on a regular basis, be that through reading our books, listening to podcasts, completing our online courses, reading the business news, watching YouTube videos, or subscribing to current affairs email digests. Even 5 minutes per day can make all the difference. Attending our events and webinars (see https://citycareerseries.clickmeeting.com) – as well as those hosted by City firms, student-focused organisations (e.g. SEO London, Bright Network, Rare Recruitment, LawCareers.Net etc.), university societies, career services, and so on – can also provide a range of opportunities to develop your understanding of current affairs and commercial concepts. I cover commercial awareness in more detail later in this handbook, but wanted to refer to it here to remind you that it's something you can start building before you start working on your applications or preparing for interviews.

Networking & Personal Brand

Some claim that nowadays, you are on average only four connections away from anyone on the planet, so you're likely closer than you might think to people who could help you do great things. With this in mind, building a positive personal brand and networking effectively can be essential if you want to succeed throughout a City career.

Building a personal brand

As a junior professional, your supervisors and other senior colleagues are often your "clients" (i.e. the people you are directly serving), and your ability to build a positive personal brand is therefore contingent on your ability to impress those colleagues. By personal brand, I mean the series of impressions and ideas that arise when people hear your name or see your face. The intangible perception others have of you based on what they have seen themselves and heard from others.

Shaping your personal brand

Your personal brand won't necessarily reflect how you *want* to be perceived, so shaping your personal brand will to some extent come down to your level of self-awareness. If you make a conscious effort to remain aware of how you are coming across, and to constantly assess how your attitude, character, abilities and approach to work are influencing others' impressions of you, then you should be well placed to deliberately adapt your actions and behaviours towards building a personal brand that aligns with how you *want* to come across.

As explained by Steve Weiner (ex-City solicitor, learning and development professional, and author of the excellent *21st Century Solicitor*): Managing brand is all about perspective, understanding the context in which you work, and modifying your behaviour where necessary. You should be questioning your behaviour all the time, perhaps by asking yourself questions like:

- Should I outwardly convey composure even if feeling overwhelmed? Do I come across as panicked? Am I using reassuring language to put people at ease, for example "I'll take care of that. Leave that with me"? How might the phrase "I don't understand" come across to others? Do I need to display a sense of urgency to please this supervisor?

- How might a messy desk with notes strewn everywhere reflect on my organisation skills? What will they think of me if I skip that training session?

- Do I need to say thank you every time I ask my secretary to do something? Did I talk down to them when I told them they had made a mistake? Is sending an email the best way to deliver good or bad news?

Ultimately, the best junior professionals are at the intersection of "competent professional", "innovative business person" and "likeable colleague and adviser". They are calm, approachable and good natured. They are great communicators. They show empathy and understanding, listen carefully and react accordingly. They never show aggression, and they are appropriately enthusiastic about every element of their job – even the rubbish bits. They also pay careful attention to how they are coming across during external (e.g. client) interactions, in the knowledge that their personal brand will also reflect on the firm.

Professionalism

Consistently demonstrating the right attitude and appropriate level of professionalism is key to cultivating a positive professional brand in a professional environment. In the junior stages of your career, you probably don't want to stand out for your appearance – including your choice of clothes, hairstyle and so on – so take stock of your surroundings and how others dress and hold themselves. You should also be wary of being too informal with seniors, as you may need to earn this right and some might perceive informality as demonstrating a lack of respect or arrogance. Always avoid arrogance, steer clear of gossip and badmouthing others (word can spread surprisingly quickly, and you may need to work with these people for years to come!), don't show panic, and never outwardly come across as bored or lacking an interest in the work or your clients. Instead, be helpful and enthusiastic, carry out your work with a smile, and become known for being punctual and reliable. As with internal interactions, always treat *everyone* with courtesy and respect, from the person in the cloakroom and the serving staff, to the receptionist, secretaries, trainees and senior lawyers. It's common decency, plus you never know who will be asked for their opinion of you come appraisal time (and fee earners may notice if you don't show the same respect to support staff).

Visibility

Personal brand is also about visibility. You might come across phenomenally well, but if very few people know you, then what's the point? You should actively seek opportunities to update, inform, educate and empower others, for example by offering to deliver presentations. On what? Well, anything from which your colleagues, and the business more generally, might benefit.

Delivering training sessions, regulatory updates, deal summaries, department insights, overviews of processes, insights into how certain challenges were surmounted, sessions covering mistakes made and how to avoid them, and so on, can help to enhance your visibility within the firm, and thus your profile, which in turn can help to establish your personal brand more widely. And this in turn can be key when it comes to cultivating a network. To conclude, Steve Weiner points out that the best professionals are: "likeable, well-connected and command high organisational visibility, both internally and externally. They seem to know or know of everyone. They always seem to have the time to chat (if not now, then later). They listen attentively whenever you talk. They ask questions to show they are listening when relevant, and they react calmly and appropriately to what others say, do or ask."

Introduction to networking

What is networking?

In short, "networking" means interacting with people to exchange information and develop professional relationships. For many people, the term "networking" brings to mind an image of a large soulless event, filled with people in formal dress drinking prosecco and trading business cards. However, networking is so much more than this. You can network in professional settings (e.g. at client events, training sessions or conferences), online (e.g. via LinkedIn, email or virtual groups), in social settings (e.g. when participating in sports teams or music ensembles, over coffee, during casual conversations etc.) and in many other contexts, each of which can be beneficial in a number of different ways. However, making a new connection is one thing. Maintaining and strengthening these relationships is a whole other challenge. It's therefore important that you develop your networking skills from an early stage, which is why I decided to cover this topic in this handbook.

How can networking benefit you?

In short: when utilised effectively, networking can offer a fantastic way to source and exchange information, access feedback and mentorship, make new connections, maintain or strengthen existing relationships, and create opportunities. As a student, networking can be essential for sourcing unique insights and important information about industries and specific firms. For example, people from within your existing network (or people you meet through networking) may be able to provide advice about a range of different careers based on their own experiences. They may help you to secure work experience or assist with your applications or interview preparation. And they could help you to make informed decisions (e.g. when deciding which firm to choose if you receive multiple offers) and provide general advice relating to your training and the work you'll be set once you start.

Moreover, networking at employer events can help you to elicit information from a firm's employees about its work, culture and key differentiators, and these insights could prove invaluable when working on your answers to firm motivation questions. You might also pick up information about the key competencies the firm expects candidates to have developed, examples of the types of questions and exercises that come up during the firm's assessment centres, and an insight into what the firm's employees actually do on a daily basis (a question that often comes up during the recruitment process).

As your career develops, networking can equip you with the contacts and information you need to capitalise upon opportunities and transition into more senior roles. At a more senior level, you might then be expected to rely on your network to attract new work and clients to the firm, at which point networking essentially becomes a marketing tool. However, networking as a junior employee can provide the foundation you need for success at a senior level, as you will climb the ranks while junior employees at client organisations also climb the ranks. Don't be short-sighted: if you have proven yourself to these people and built solid relationships over time, they will likely be more willing to send work your way in the future. For this reason, some firms allocate budgets to juniors to encourage them to network with lower-level employees of potential (and actual) client businesses.

In addition, if you ever want to move to another office, work for another firm or change careers altogether, your network could be essential for helping you to discover the opportunities available, get a foot in the door, and hit the ground running. It's also highly likely that you will end up working with or for people from within your network throughout your career, and networking from an early stage can help to lay the foundations for positive working relationships further down the line. In general, the longer your history with people, the more likely it is that they will be willing to help you. And if you've already built up a rapport, some good will and a degree of trust with a colleague or collaborator, you'll be in a great place when it comes to tapping up those connections later on. So always strive to make a positive first impression, and make the effort to keep in touch with your connections. Even something as simple as sharing one of their LinkedIn posts or dropping them a congratulatory email can have a tangible positive impact on your relationship with them.

Building your network

As a student, your "network" is probably far broader than you may think. It theoretically includes your family, friends of family members, your childhood friends, your school friends and university peers (including those in other years and even alumni), your tutors, lecturers and career advisers, and the people you've met at networking events and during insight days and internships. Then when you start work, your network will expand almost immediately to include other graduates and colleagues in your team. As you carry out more and more work, your network will further expand to include colleagues in other departments and international offices, representatives from the firm's clients, and individuals from firms that work alongside (or opposite) your firm. This might include bankers, lawyers, accountants, consultants, regulators and an almost infinite range of other stakeholders.

How can you meet more people and build your network? Well, according to Steve Weiner: "where possible, try to build a rapport outside the rigid hierarchical constraints of the firm. Doing so means a senior colleague can become less than just a name at the foot of an email and more a genuine contact in the organisation". With this in mind, try to get involved in non-fee earning activities. Volunteer to contribute to corporate social responsibility programmes and pro bono initiatives. Join committees and employee networks. Offer to help with business development or client relationship management. Join sports teams or music ensembles. Attend team training sessions, lunches and socials. And so on.

It's also important to remember that networking is not just about what *you* can gain from somebody else. It's as much about assisting others. Networking should be mutually beneficial, and this is something that the most effective networkers are well aware of. For this reason, you shouldn't wait until you have a favour to ask before connecting with someone; build the relationship without a goal in mind and – if at all possible – seek out opportunities (professional or otherwise) to offer help to others whenever it's needed. This approach will help you to expand your network. And if your network is full of people who you've helped without (initially) seeking anything in return, you'll be very well positioned if *you* need help at a later stage.

Practical tip: consider maintaining a spreadsheet of who you've met, their contact details (or LinkedIn profile URL if you've corresponded via LinkedIn), how you met them (e.g. via an introduction), when and where you spoke to them, what you discussed, and how they might be able to help. You never know when you'll want to get back in touch in the future, and if you meet dozens (or hundreds) of people in the interim, you might struggle to keep track of names and the relevance of each interaction. Having a database of contacts to hand has certainly helped me on countless occasions!

Building your confidence

Let's be honest, networking can be intimidating. The fear of knockbacks, rejection and making a fool of ourselves can cause us to be hesitant, or to give up altogether. This is perfectly natural, and (almost) everybody feels this way when they start networking for the first time. However, the only way to get rid of the fear of networking is to *go out and do it.*

Back when I was touring as a full-time musician, every time we visited a city for the first time, we knew we had to convince at least 10-15 people to show up to watch us play, otherwise the venue wouldn't invite us back again next time. As a result, we used to go to each new city a few hours before soundcheck and walk around shopping centres, town squares and any other busy public spaces we could find, then approach groups of people and talk to them about our music. And it was terrifying. Initially. However, as we started to do this hour after hour, day after day, the fear started to subside, the knockbacks seemed less personal, and the whole process became more natural. We no longer hesitated before approaching groups, as we were no longer worried about the outcome. We didn't focus on the possibility of a negative interaction, as we had enjoyed enough positive interactions to know that it would likely be ok. And we simply trusted that it would all be worthwhile, in the end.

As a student, you can go through a similar process simply by attending as many career fairs and employer events as possible – virtual or otherwise – and just having a variety of short conversations with new people. Don't worry too much initially about saying anything profound. Just aim to build your confidence, and the rest will come. You'll naturally pick up on and learn from the positive things that other, more seasoned networkers are doing, and can then start to adopt some of these techniques yourself.

How to network successfully

Since publishing the very first edition of this handbook, fresh out of university, I have had countless experiences networking on the "other side of the table". Representing firms, rather than networking with firms. And as a result, I've picked up a number of insights that will hopefully help you to improve your approach.

Getting into the right mindset

You should *always* follow up any potential leads and *never* discount somebody that you haven't met before. I can't stress this enough. If a friend tells you that they know someone who might be able to help or collaborate with you, meet them, even if you can't immediately see why the meeting might be relevant. You just never know. Some of the best opportunities that have come my way have resulted from a meeting that – at the time – didn't seem to have any particular relevance to my professional life.

How to approach a prospective contact

Securing direct introductions

If somebody recommends that you speak to one of their contacts, ask that person to introduce you to that contact *directly* (e.g. by copying you into an email to that contact and explaining who you are and why they are making the introduction). The "direct introduction" exponentially increases your chances of receiving a response, as the contact likely won't feel comfortable ignoring you, in the knowledge that this could reflect negatively on them to the person who made the introduction.

Finding an "in"

If you're reaching out to a potential new connection but aren't able to secure an introduction from somebody, try to find some kind of shared experience to mention in your initial message to that person. In other words, do your research so that you can find an "in". This "in" might be that you both studied the same course at the same university, worked at the same summer camp, attended the same church, or grew up abroad in the same country. Anything that can help them to remember what it was like to be in your shoes. Of course, it would be unrealistic to expect a 100% response rate, but this approach can at least help to shift the odds in your favour. You could even use the LinkedIn search filters to find people whose experiences are somehow connected to your own, and then reach out to them in priority.

Reaching out to a prospective contact

Once you've found your "in", make sure you highlight this (e.g. in a LinkedIn connection request) so that the person knows why you have decided to approach *them* in particular. Next, explain what you are approaching them about. For example, do they work at a firm that you're in the process of applying to, or where you have an upcoming internship? Finally, be sure to explain what you're looking for (e.g. advice), then end with a clear call to action. This might be, for example, a request for some written insights, a quick phone call, or a coffee.

Throughout this process, remember that the people you are contacting are likely very busy, slightly (or very!) stressed out, and juggling a wide variety of personal and professional responsibilities. Demonstrate that you're aware of this, you respect their time, and you'll appreciate any help whatsoever. Tying into this theme, do everything you can to make the other person's role as easy as possible and don't ask too much of them, as this can show a lack of respect. Don't ask for 2 hours of their time, ask for 10 minutes and then take it from there. Offer to meet them whenever and wherever suits them best. And if they do meet with you, at least *offer* to buy them a coffee to show your appreciation. I've genuinely had people whom I've never met or spoken to ask me to proofread a lengthy application late at night, with a follow up message to say that the application deadline is actually the next morning! Needless to say, this didn't come across well.

> **Practical tip:** if somebody does agree to speak with you at some point in the future, send them a calendar invite and include in the invite a few brief notes reminding them of who you are, how you met, and what you wanted to discuss with them. That way, they're less likely to forget about the call/meeting (or to delete the calendar invite having forgotten who you are).

How to interact with others

Your narrative

It's all well and good perfecting the craft of breaking into group discussions or persuading someone to speak to you. However, you also need to give some thought as to what you're actually going to *say* when people do speak to you. Think about your narrative. Your elevator pitch. What you will say if somebody picks up the phone and says "tell me about yourself?, or "so, how can I help?". In these situations, you should clearly and concisely articulate what you're currently doing and what you are looking for. It could be as simple as: "Hi, I'm Jake, I'm a 2nd year Law & Business student, and I'm looking to learn more about Firm ABC as I'm interested in pursuing a career at a large City law firm." Or, if you are looking for more specific insights or information, be ready to clearly explain what you already know, and the knowledge gaps you're looking to fill.

Asking questions

According to author of *21st Century Solicitor* Steve Weiner: "networking for juniors means less networking (the verb) and more cultivating a network (the noun). And, surprise surprise, it isn't rocket science. It is what you should be doing every day: internal and external relationship-building, being calm, light-hearted, likeable, bright and charming. And the key to this lies in showing a genuine interest in the people you meet, both in your professional capacity, and in your non-professional capacity as a human being. People generally like to talk about themselves, so asking questions is a good way to show you are interested and to build trust and credibility. And asking open questions can give you material to ask further questions as the conversation develops".

If possible, look up people you may be meeting – and their companies – in advance, as this can give helpful background that enables you to tailor your questions and conversation topics accordingly. On that note, avoid questions that you could easily find the answers to online (from personal experience, I know this can be boring and even frustrating for the professionals present), and tailor your questions to the role and seniority of those you are networking with. If you're talking to a partner, don't start asking them about application deadlines or the mechanics of training contract seat selection. Take advantage of their knowledge and experience! Perhaps ask about their career: what has kept them at the firm for so long, how has their role changed over time, what is their favourite thing about the job, what are their career highlights, what is the biggest challenge they have faced etc. If the person then starts talking about their career, think of follow-up questions. For example, if they say they moved between firms or departments, you could ask why they chose to do so, and what differences they noticed in the subsequent role.

Conversely, there's no point asking a trainee or analyst what has kept them in the role for so long. Perhaps ask junior employees about why they chose the firm, what they have found particularly challenging, what they have really enjoyed, or how their role in practice compares to what they had imagined before joining. Moreover, don't waste graduate recruiters' time by asking questions that you could find out following a quick Google, as this won't show much initiative. Instead, you could ask about the work that you might encounter on a vacation scheme, or the nature of the training throughout the graduate scheme.

Following up

If possible, follow up your meeting with a thank you. This could be by email or via LinkedIn, or (if it is someone internal) you could briefly pop into their office. Perhaps mention something specific that you talked about during the original interaction (this will help them to remember you), or share a related article or resource. Doing so creates another networking "touchpoint", which increases the likelihood of that person remembering you. The more touchpoints you accumulate with someone, the more familiar you will become with one another, which is all part of maintaining and strengthening relationships.

Practical tip: when reaching out to someone via LinkedIn for the first time, send a personalised message with your connection request. In the connection request, remind them who you are and how you met. Senior professionals will likely receive hundreds of anonymous connection requests per month, so a personalised message can help you stand out. Conversely, failing to personalise a connection request can make you appear lazy and unprofessional, which may result in your request being ignored. In addition, including a message with your connection request means you'll always be able to refer back to when and why you originally connected with someone (as the message will then sit in your LinkedIn message chain with that person).

Formal networking events

Preparation

As mentioned, if you know in advance who you'll be meeting at a formal networking event (e.g. a dinner hosted by a firm or networking drinks), perhaps do some prior research. See if someone you'll be meeting has published thought leadership articles on LinkedIn or through their firm's website, and if so, give them a read. If you later approach that person, tell them you enjoyed one of their articles and ask them a couple of thoughtful follow-up questions. They'll likely be flattered and very impressed. Plus they'll also remember you, at least for a while.

Practical tip: when speaking to employees, make sure that you bring a pen and paper with you and take notes! You may not interview at that firm for another year and a half, so will likely otherwise forget all the insights you have worked so hard to pick up. People won't think it's weird if you write while they talk, as long as you maintain some level of eye contact and actually respond if they ask you questions. In fact, when I represented firms at career fairs and networking events, I sometimes felt like my time was being wasted if people I spoke to *didn't* take notes, as I knew they would likely forget our conversation as soon as they moved onto the next employee or firm.

Professionalism

Make sure you dress appropriately (first impressions and all that), and respect those around you. In a group scenario, don't monopolise a particular person by trying to dominate the conversation if others are waiting patiently for their turn. This can come across negatively to all involved, which won't buy you much good will. In contrast, when I was networking with students and one was gracious enough to take a step back and let others have their turn, I would go out of my way to try to make time for them again later in the evening.

Practical tip: if you want to talk to a range of people, but find yourself stuck in one particular conversation, try to find a polite way to excuse yourself and move on. For example, you could say you need to grab a drink (although you should probably then offer a drink to the person/people you're speaking to, and just hope they decline!). Or perhaps say you're heading to the loo (and hope the conversation has moved on by the time you return!).

Keeping an open mind

Don't avoid talking to someone just because you think they're too junior to be helpful, or won't have useful insights. This ties into the point made above about not discounting people you haven't met: you can't be sure until you've tried! For example, I attended a City law firm's campus presentation during my very first week at university. After the presentation, almost everybody swarmed the partners, so I went to speak to one of the trainees. As nobody else was around, this gave me a solid hour to ask a broad range of questions and gave us the chance to build up a decent rapport. He ended up helping me with my application and meeting me for a coffee when I attended an insight day. Now, almost a decade later, we're still friends. In fact, we recently attended each other's weddings! You. Just. Never. Know.

Reflection, Preparation & Application Strategy

Preparation is key. Completing strong applications can take a great deal of time, as can preparing sufficiently for interviews and internships. Application deadlines may well overlap with university assignment deadlines and exam revision periods, whilst I have heard many examples of people being offered interviews with only a couple of days' notice. It's therefore advisable that you start preparing as early as possible. This chapter focuses on general tips and insights relating to applications and preparing for interviews. Later in this handbook, we then cover specific types of application and interview questions in much more detail.

Self-reflection

We've teamed up with ex-City graduate recruitment manager and acclaimed career coach Hannah Salton, who has provided key insights and top tips throughout this book (just look out for the orange boxes). Below, Hannah has set out her thoughts on the importance of self-reflection in the context of graduate recruitment processes. Over to Hannah…

Our career preferences are complex and tend to balance a range of different (and sometimes conflicting) desires and needs. Our preferences can also be deeply affected by external factors such as the opinions and experiences of friends, family and society more broadly. Some of these influences may be subconscious, meaning it can be hard to detangle precisely what it is that you want.

Sometimes it may feel that everyone else from your university course knows exactly what they want to do in life. It may also feel as if everyone around you already has a graduate job in place and it's therefore only you that is still looking. In reality, it's rare for an undergraduate to have clear, fixed career objectives. And of those that think they have found clarity early on, it's likely that many will find that their choices do not quite align with their expectations.

Many who have strong opinions about what they want to do very early on can end up limiting themselves by not taking the time to explore alternate career paths. This can sometimes lead to them following a career path based more on the most obvious or common choice, rather than making a well-thought out and suitably researched decision. It might sound clichéd, but remember you're not in competition with anyone but yourself. Feeling intimidated by your peers' success (or even motivated by their failures) presents an unnecessary distraction. Don't get side-tracked by comparing your journey to the journeys of others.

How can "knowing myself" help me find the right career?

So, how exactly will knowing yourself help you to find the right job? Firstly, being aware of your values, strengths and drivers can help you to identify and articulate what is most important to you. Equipped with this knowledge, you can try and focus your research and applications towards companies and roles that are more likely to align with you, which will increase the chances of finding a job that will give you higher levels of day to day satisfaction.

Secondly, having greater self-awareness will provide you with an invaluable toolkit that will help prepare you for success during graduate recruitment processes. Throughout a typical job selection process, you will be expected to demonstrate a solid understanding of yourself – including your skills and strengths – and to talk effectively about any professional or voluntary experience that you have accumulated.

Your values and drivers are also likely to be explored or assessed, along with your motivation for choosing to apply to the specific role or industry. Your ability to clearly articulate answers to questions such as "why do you want to work here?" or "what has motivated you to become a lawyer?" is imperative, both on application forms and during interviews. Values are personal and deep-rooted, so can strongly affect whether or not you enjoy your work. For this reason, it is important to take your values into account when deciding which careers and employers to pursue. If a type of career or an employer's values do not align with your own values, you could find yourself becoming frustrated and disillusioned with your career and lose the motivation to maintain high standards of performance over time. At the very least, it is essential that the companies you apply for do not violate or contradict your most important values.

How can I tell what a company's values are?

The first place to look is the company's website or careers portal. Companies – particularly larger ones – are much more open and transparent about their values than they were 10 years ago, as they recognise the benefit of attracting candidates whose values align with those of the company. This is because values often drive culture, and working environments have a huge influence on how happy and successful we are at work.

Manifestations of these values can sometimes be obvious in the language and wording used by firms when talking about their businesses on their websites. For example, if a company shares a lot of insights around training and professional development – along with clear examples of how staff have benefited from its internal training programmes – the company is likely to value the professional development of its employees. Newer companies with more informal cultures may try to get this across by using a friendly or informal tone of voice in their communications. It's not uncommon for smaller companies – when wanting to come across as friendly and approachable – to have employer profiles that include "fun facts" such as employees' favourite crisp flavours. In a similar vein, many new tech start-ups try and create the image of a light-hearted and inclusive culture by sharing details of an office games room or company pet.

How might your interests be relevant?

You may have some interests that are more obviously linked to certain types of careers, in which case linking your own interests to a particular career paths may be fairly easy. In many cases however, you may need to reflect a little deeper to work out how your interests could help point to a possible career direction. Think about your interests in broad terms. For example, what subjects or modules have you enjoyed most whilst studying? Which industries, sectors, products and companies do you most enjoy reading about? If money were no object, what type of work would you love to do?

While certain interests may not yield many direct employment opportunities (being a cheese and wine taster doesn't yield too many entry level job opportunities!), recognising that you have a strong interest in politics, travelling or fashion may well steer you towards exploring a career path that enables you to discover roles you didn't previously know existed. It's unlikely that you will find a job that is 100% encompassing of your hobby; but certain career choices may be more aligned to your general interests. It's also worth recognising the difference between a hobby that you enjoy sporadically for pleasure, versus one that you would be happy to pursue in a structured way on a daily basis. For example, some people love doing yoga once a week, but doing it every day as a yoga instructor and relying on it as your main source of income may well eliminate the fun!

Understanding your priorities

To help work out what you are looking for, it can be useful to create a shopping list of your most important career ingredients, as knowing which elements are important to you will help when you start to navigate the vast and complex job market. Once you have identified these, you should start to consider the types of role that might suit you best, as well as the types of employers that appeal to you the most. Below, I tackle some frequently asked questions and dilemmas that graduates commonly face when trying to work out what types of companies they want to apply to.

Should I join a structured graduate programme?

Structured graduate programmes

Many graduates like the idea of first embarking upon a structured training programme, as opposed to commencing a standalone role within a company (i.e. a role that isn't part of a structured graduate programme). One of the benefits of doing so is that there may be more opportunities to gain a further academic or professional qualification whilst working, with your employer covering the cost. For example, some professional services firms have inbuilt accounting training for graduate programmes where the aim is to qualify as an accountant. Some HR or Marketing graduate programmes also have a built in CIPD (Chartered Institute of Personnel Development) or CIM (Chartered Institute of Marketing) qualification as part of the programme. However, bear in mind that many employers include "claw back" clauses in their employment contracts which mean that employees who voluntarily leave within a certain time frame after completing a qualification may have to repay some or all of the cost of the relevant qualification.

If a specific academic qualification is a requirement before joining a graduate programme, a graduate employer will most likely cover the required tuition fees for you. For example, most large corporate law firms pay the tuition fees plus a basic living allowance to graduates who need to complete prerequisite qualifications such as the Legal Practice Course and Graduate Diploma in Law before commencing their training contracts. In addition to any formal professional or academic qualifications, companies that offer graduate training programmes are often more likely to have in place a comprehensive range of internal or external training courses for employees of all levels of seniority, covering both technical and soft skills. This means there may be more opportunities to continue your professional development once the programme ends.

Standalone roles

Whilst there are exceptions, in contrast most standalone roles tend to involve a more ad-hoc approach to training, with much of the training being "on the job". Whether this is better for you is simply a matter of preference. A standalone role may also allow for greater flexibility and freedom, for example by giving you more say over the roles and responsibilities involved in your day-to-day work. Standalone roles may also better suit you if you are confident on the exact type of role you want. For example, if you are certain that you want to work specifically in digital advertising, joining a boutique agency that only carries out digital advertising work might be preferable to spending two years on a rotational graduate programme that requires you to try out other areas of the business (e.g. operations, human resources, sales etc.). Finally, graduates who have already accumulated a few years of work experience might prefer a standalone role, as entering the structured (and sometimes restrictive) world of graduate programmes might feel like taking a step back.

Large versus small employers

What are the main differences between large companies (including global City firms) and smaller companies (including high street or regional firms)? Understanding these can help you identify which types of companies might suit you best.

What do we mean by "large" or "small" employers?

The specific differences between companies of different sizes will vary a great deal, but there are certain characteristics that tend to align with organisations of similar sizes. In this context, by "size", we generally mean the number of employees in your place of work. A large international firm may have very small offices in certain locations that are run more like small companies, whilst a smaller regional company may have only one office, but employ a large number of people in that office (meaning it could feel more like working at a large international firm).

What are the typical fundamental differences?

Larger companies tend to have more formal or structured training programmes (discussed above), but may also have a reputation for being slightly more bureaucratic, more hierarchal, and less flexible in terms of the work that is allocated to employees of different levels of seniority. This can result in a general lack of transparency, as well as juniors receiving lower levels of responsibility and less exposure to high quality work. Large corporations can sometimes be slower to implement change than smaller, more agile organisations, which can be frustrating at times, especially in relation to outdated IT systems!

On the plus side, larger companies tend to have in place a strong infrastructure to support employees internally. For example, they often have specific teams that help with day to day administrative tasks such as submitting expenses, organising business travel, and other basic operational requirements. This can help to free up time for employees to focus on the more relevant and commercial aspects of their roles.

Smaller companies may lack the same levels of administrative support (especially in start-ups or small boutique firms), although you might find you are given more flexibility and scope to work across a diverse range of projects. This could mean that you have opportunities to gain higher levels of exposure to a broader range of tasks and clients, enabling you to learn more in a practical manner and at a quicker rate. This can equip you with a broad range of practical business skills, which is useful if you are interested in one day running your own business.

Many people believe that starting your career at a large, well known company can prove an advantage for the rest of your career, as being successfully employed by a recognised and reputable company may reassure future employers of your employability, which can open your options when you're looking to move to your next opportunity. There is some truth to this in certain contexts, but it very much depends on the nature of your next move. Larger companies also often pay higher salaries than smaller companies, tend to offer more job security, and provide benefits such as gym access and private health insurance (although this varies wildly across industries). However, smaller companies might offer equity as part of their compensation packages, as well as greater (and quicker) career progression, which could act as a spring board into a more senior role elsewhere further down the line. The lower levels of bureaucracy and flatter hierarchies that tend to exist in smaller companies, coupled with the fact that you tend to feel less "anonymous" in a small team, are also differences that are worth considering.

Finally, if you really want to travel and work internationally, large corporations may offer more opportunities to do so, including opportunities to work with international clients or in international offices. However, these companies may offer little choice or flexibility in terms of where or when you travel, which could have a big impact on your personal life. For this reason, although frequent international travel can sound glamorous at first, it may not be something you want in the long run. Also bear in mind that "travel" might mean travelling to other regional offices or client sites in the UK (a far cry from the Cayman Islands!), in some cases for up to 5 days a week (which can be very disruptive).

Graduate intake size

Companies often give an indication as to how many graduates they take on each year. Large or small numbers are not objectively good or bad, but you may want to consider your preference. A large graduate intake hopefully indicates that the company has solid procedures in place to help manage the development of the cohort. You would likely assume that this includes comprehensive training courses and adequate resources to manage any issues relating to human resources or professional development. A large graduate intake should also mean that you'll have access to a wider immediate network of like-minded peers, which can enable you to build personal and professional relationships with a greater number of people, many of whom you're likely to stay in touch with throughout your career. There may also be a greater variety of – and more investment into – social events, sports clubs and interest clubs.

However, you might feel more anonymous in a larger intake, and might have a less personalised experience during the training programme. Moreover, allocation to departments or roles may be more of a numbers game, aligning to company needs rather than your preferences (although it's worth nothing that even with small intakes, business needs generally dictate where graduates are placed). Being part of a smaller cohort may enable you to build more intimate relationships with your fellow graduates, and get to know everyone that joins at the same time as you. Some people would assume there would be more competition with a smaller intake, with fewer of the most desirable permanent positions available at the end. However, in my experience, there's no consistent correlation with this.

Why I left the City

I left the City for two key reasons. Firstly, I wanted more control over my time. By "control", I don't mean that I wanted to work fewer hours. Instead, I mean that I wanted more oversight over what work was potentially coming my way (rather than having to drop everything at a moment's notice), plus the ability to turn work down. Why? So that it would be easier to plan my social/family life and to properly commit to non-work-related events and responsibilities. I probably work far more hours on average now – as a self-employed business owner – than I did in the City, but I have ultimate control over those hours, which makes a huge difference to me. Note that my son was born towards the end of my training contract, which I think fed into this desire; things may have been different had I started working in the City in my early 20s, before having children.

Secondly, I wanted to be able to see the direct impact that my personal contributions were having, which I found difficult when working on huge legal matters with dozens of other advisers. For some, "impact" means working on multimillion pound, high-profile, headline-grabbing projects, which is a totally reasonable interpretation. But for me, I cared less about the prestige. Instead, I now find myself really enjoying working with founders of small, early-stage businesses, where my advice has a real *perceivable* impact on those businesses. It doesn't matter to me that most people haven't heard of those businesses (for now!), or that the monetary sums involved are comparatively small. Of course, money and job security are also important considerations. But for me, it was worth sacrificing some of my income and accepting lower levels of job security to have the career I wanted. It's simply a matter of personal preference.

Where can you seek out potentially relevant roles?

Where can you seek out potentially relevant roles?

Once you've figured out the type of company you want to join, you'll then need to research into the roles available. To assist with this, here are some of Hannah's recommended resources for finding out about potential careers and firms:

Times Top 100 and Guardian UK 300

Publications like these are great for listening out the most popular employers that students want to work for. Be mindful that these rankings are normally based on student perception e.g. which employers undergraduate students pick as their preferred employers, rather than an objective analysis of the best graduate jobs.

LinkedIn

You can use LinkedIn to research into the employers that graduates from your university and course tend to join, as well as the roles they take on. If you find an employer that you like the look of, you can then use the LinkedIn "similar companies" search function to find similar companies/options. Use this for inspiration, but don't restrict yourself too much: just because an alumnus from your course hasn't previously joined your preferred employer doesn't mean you won't have a chance.

Job boards

Search online for graduate jobs in your chosen fields. Be mindful that job adverts can sometimes (often) be confusing, particularly if you have no experience working in the relevant industry. Don't be put off by complicated language or unfamiliar acronyms; it's ok if you don't understand the detail in job descriptions, especially when you're new to researching.

Graduate specific job sites

Graduate job platforms such as BrightNetwork.co.uk and Prospects.co.uk can provide useful points of reference. Many of these will compile employment opportunities that are listed throughout the resources mentioned above. Try and drill down into less obvious employers too, by using niche job boards; there are specific job boards for all kind of focuses, for example AngelList for start-ups. You can also filter by criteria such as location, for example if you're looking for jobs in a specific region.

Hannah Salton is a qualified executive coach, career consultant and former City graduate recruitment manager. Together, we run a bespoke career coaching programme designed to help students and graduates secure highly competitive City roles. **Visit www.hannahsalton.co.uk/blog for more information, as well as a range of unique tips and insights relating to the City recruitment process.**

Your application strategy

Progressing through the application stage is typically the hardest part of any recruitment process, as this is where the vast majority of candidates are rejected. You might have a 1 in 50 (or 1 in 100+) chance of getting through to interview, but once you're there, your odds are significantly higher. However, these statistics are only relevant if "luck" is the key factor. And although luck may play some part in you getting through to the interview stage, it's certainly not a key factor in the vast majority of cases. It's about hard work, dedication, academic consistency, accumulating experiences, articulating skills effectively, and working relentlessly on your research and application writing. With that in mind, hopefully the tips, insights and principles covered throughout this chapter and beyond will go some way to demonstrating how you can ace your applications. Note that this section focuses on how to approach your applications more generally; we then cover specific types of application questions in much more detail later in this handbook.

What makes a good application?

So, what makes a good application? This is a question I have been considering for the better part of a decade: first as a student, then as an author of career-centric handbooks, later as a trainee solicitor and practising lawyer, and more recently as a career coach and event speaker. I've probably reviewed close to 1,000 applications in my time, and it can be difficult to identify any one thing that distinguishes the good, from the bad and the ugly. However, I'll now cover a few general tips to keep in mind.

Avoid generic answers

Now, you've probably been told repeatedly to avoid "generic" answers, but may be less sure how to do so. Well, matching your terminology to a firm's terminology can be a good start. If firms highlight specific sought after skills (e.g. on their websites), try to cover each of these in your application, and use the same wording they do (for example, refer to "organisational skills" rather than "time-management skills", if this is the firm's approach). In addition, if you're referencing a particular department or practice area, again, use the same terminology that the firm does (e.g. does the firm state that it has a "finance" practice or a "banking" practice?). More broadly, you need to make sure that your answers are personal and authentic wherever possible. For example, when discussing your motivations, link these back to your own experiences and learnings. And when discussing competencies and skills, use *personal* examples to demonstrate how you have developed and utilised these.

Write clearly and concisely

One issue I come across time and time again involves candidates writing applications in the same style as university essays. However, this isn't how people communicate in client-facing roles, so avoid writing too academically. Instead, answer questions using clear, concise language, prioritising plain English over jargon where possible. After all, the first person to read your application will typically be a graduate recruiter, who might not be familiar with technical concepts and jargon. And if they don't understand your application, then you're less likely to progress to the next stage.

Answer the specific questions you are asked

It's important that you quickly get to the point when answering questions, and then *stick to the point*. Especially when the word limit is tight. However – and this is another common issue – candidates often fail to properly read the questions they're asked, which can result in them going off topic and missing important aspects of what's being asked.

> **Practical tip:** perhaps highlight or underline key aspects of multifaceted questions at the start, to make absolutely sure you cover every aspect of each question. And then stay on track!

In this context, copying and pasting answers from other applications can really trip you up, as firms tend to ask questions that seem fairly identical on an initial read, but actually have nuanced differences. For example, one firm might ask about work experiences, positions of responsibility and achievements, whereas another might ask about positions of responsibility and extracurricular activities. If you talk about work experience in the latter scenario, then it will be clear that you haven't properly read the question. Other examples that trip students up include "why do you want to work for us?"(which focuses on *your* motivation to train there) vs. "why do clients choose to work with us?" (which focuses on the firm's competitive advantages and client retention strategies), and "which relevant skills have you developed?" (which focuses on your competencies) vs. "how will your skills help you to succeed in the role?" (which focuses more on what the role involves and why the skills are relevant).

Structure

It goes without saying that spelling and grammar should be absolutely on point. However, structure is equally important. If your structure is all over the place, your application will be more difficult to read, which might result in a graduate recruiter giving up before reaching the end. This could also indicate that you would struggle to draft concise, well-written client notes and research reports if hired, which doesn't give the greatest first impression. In addition, a weak structure might lead to you including new points that overlap with or duplicate existing points, which is counterintuitive when you're trying to make every word count. For example, if you are discussing your motivation for wanting to work at a particular firm, don't mention training at the start, in the middle and at the end of your answer. Perhaps have a section dedicated to the development of employees, thus avoiding the risk of repeating yourself and coming across as unable to write coherently.

> **Practical tip:** one trick to help ensure that you write with a solid structure in place is to write out headings before you start writing each of your answers (even short answers). This can help to ensure that you don't lose sight of structure – and what needs to be covered – during the writing process, and therefore increase the chances of your answers remaining logical and cohesive. You can always then delete the headings before submitting the application.

Seek advice and feedback

It can really help to seek advice and feedback from the get-go. If you have not yet written applications, perhaps visit your university's career service, or meet with friends and family members if they have experience applying to or working for similar firms. They may be able to provide an insight into what firms are expecting from your application answers (although bear in mind that their insights may be less helpful if they work in completely different industries). Career departments also tend to offer application checks as one of their services. When this is the case, use them! In addition, look out for firm presentations on campus that relate to the application process. Who better to secure advice from than the firm to which you are applying?

It can also be really beneficial to have your applications proofread by multiple sources over an extended period, regardless of whether they have any legal experience. Sometimes you simply need a fresh pair of eyes. You're probably more likely to miss mistakes or structural issues than a person taking a fresh look at your application, as once you've been buried in an application for an extended period of time, you're at risk of reading what you think you wrote (or intended to write), as opposed to what you actually wrote. This is something that happened to me over and over again whilst working on my own applications and writing my books. So I learnt to accept any help I was offered from people willing to proofread sections.

Do not lie

It's fine to present yourself in the best possible light on applications and during interviews. However, never lie. There's a good chance you'll get found out, if not immediately, then further down the line. And firms won't want to hire liars, especially in highly regulated industries. For example, if you state that you are proficient in a different language, make sure you remember how to speak it when you attend an interview: I have heard stories of interviewers suddenly switching to a different language mid-interview to check whether the candidate really could speak the languages they claimed to know. Don't get caught out!

How many applications should I submit?

Many candidates ask how many applications they should submit, but there is no definitive answer. I personally believe that the number of applications you submit should depend on two factors:

1. How much time you are willing and able to commit to each application

Sending out 3 or 4 thoroughly researched and well written applications is more likely to result in you being offered interviews than if you send out 100 poorly researched, badly written applications.

2. How competitive it is to get the job for which you are applying

For competitive internships or training programmes (e.g. programmes for which perhaps 1 in 20+ applicants tend to receive an offer), you really should hedge your bets. Consider sending out at least 10-12 *high quality* applications – if not more – and perhaps apply to a range of different types of firms, for example international, national, regional and boutique firms. You never know which type of firm happens to be looking for someone just like you.

On that note, be realistic. If a firm states that it only recruits candidates with top grades or extensive experience, consider whether you meet these criteria (or have relevant extenuating circumstances). If not, perhaps focus at least some of your efforts elsewhere, whilst trying to improve your grades and accumulate more experience. And even if you believe you tick all of the boxes, applying to only one or two firms is a risky strategy, as rejection can sometimes come down to bad luck (more on this below).

In addition, certain opportunities might only be available to students that are studying particular degrees or have reached specific stages in their degrees (and some might even be open only to graduates). Moreover, some employers recruit on a rolling basis – meaning that they assess candidates and make offers as and when they receive applications – which can lead to the real risk that spaces will fill up before their application deadlines. Ultimately, there is no point wasting time on an application only to discover that you are not eligible to apply or that all the places have been taken, so do your research!

Use a word processor

When writing applications, I recommend that you draft your application answers in a word processor such as Microsoft Word (rather than writing them directly within the relevant online portal), and this is for a few key reasons. Firstly, if an employer's application portal crashes or the internet drops, you could end up losing all the work you have completed up until that point. You can mitigate this risk by writing your answers in a Microsoft Word document (and regularly saving that document), then pasting your completed answers into the application portal right at the end. Secondly, by writing your answers in Microsoft Word, over time you will build up a bank of answers, which you can then use as inspiration when answering subsequent application questions. I'm not suggesting that you lazily copy/paste answers into other application forms however; it's always essential that you properly tailor any existing wording to the specific questions you are asked, and use up as much of the allocated word count as possible.

On that note, writing in Microsoft Word means you can easily check the word count as you go, which can help to keep your answers concise and avoid you having to later go through the lengthy process of cutting out hundreds of words (we've all been there with university essays!). In addition, writing in Word means you'll have a record of your application. if you don't keep a record of your application, you won't be able to remind yourself of what you included if you're later invited to interview. And this could be problematic, as if your application mentions (for example) a specific news story or a deal that the firm has advised on, you'll likely want to carry out some additional research to refresh your memory in case your interviewer brings it up. Finally, if you write your answers in Microsoft Word, you can make at least some use of the in-built spell checker. You shouldn't fully rely on it (as it doesn't always pick up errors), but it should at least pick up on the more obvious errors.

Dealing with rejection

Even with the right grades, highly developed skill sets and strong application answers, almost everyone will experience some form of rejection from time to time. But this isn't necessarily a bad thing. Rejection has actually been an incredibly important part of my own learning process: learning what not to do can be an essential part of truly understanding what works well. Plus, sometimes rejection may just come down to bad luck. A graduate recruiter may happen to have read your application at the end of a very long day, and failed to pick up on some of the key points. Your application might have popped up right after the greatest application ever written, and simply not come across as well in comparison. A firm may be looking for a very specific type of candidate or degree background. Some firms are stricter than others when it comes to your university (or even school) grades. Some firms will even blanket reject applications if they come across a single typo. You just don't know.

I've been rejected on dozens (if not hundreds) of occasions over the past decade. I was rejected after my very first phone interview, but the feedback I received helped to transform my approach to boosting my employability (I had only given non-academic examples to back up my skill development, whereas they were looking for a broader mix of experiences). I was rejected by 12 out of 12 investment banks in my first year, but kept with it and finally secured a Spring Week in my second year. I was rejected by law firms for open days, campus ambassador positions, internships and training contracts, but eventually managed to secure a training contract with my first choice firm. On that note, Freshfields even rejected me for a campus ambassador role *after* offering me a training contract! I also had barely any luck when applying to consulting firms, but now work as a freelance consultant. I couldn't always clearly identify why I was rejected. It just happens. However, if you *are* receiving dozens of rejections and having no success, it's worth having another think about the structure and content of your applications (or at least having them proofread by someone else), as well as whether your work experience and grades meet any benchmarks set by the firms you're applying to.

> **Hannah Salton's top tips for dealing with rejection**
>
> There are so many reasons why people get rejected from roles. Sometimes it's because the role has already been filled. Sometimes the volume of applications is disproportionately high, so not everybody's application gets looked at. Sometimes the vacancy is filled internally. Sometimes the business demand changes, so there are fewer hires needed. Of course, sometimes you're just not right for the role. A big mistake candidates often make though, is assuming that the outcome of rejection categorically means that they are not good enough. This could be the case, however don't make assumptions when there are so many other external factors affecting whether or not you get hired. If you're feeling overwhelmed with your job search, here are a few key things to bear in mind:
>
> **1. Stay present:** getting overly caught up in narratives (I'll never get a job, I'll always be rejected) can feel overwhelming and divert our attention from potential solutions. Take some deep breaths, remind yourself where you are now, acknowledge that almost everybody has been rejected multiple times, and move forward.
>
> **2. Recognise the context and try to seek some perspective:** most professional problems are temporary, even if they don't feel this way at the time. Looking for a job can feel all-consuming, but it's unlikely you'll remember this as significant in a few years' time. Try to identify examples of when past worries have evaporated over time, and keep your challenges in perspective.
>
> **3. Remember what is constant:** life can feel busy and hectic, and with most of us moving jobs and changing career more frequently these days, the highs and lows can sometimes feel excessively turbulent. Remind yourself what is constant in your life – whether this is a hobby, your family, or even exercise – as this can make even the scariest of situations more bearable.
>
> **4. Take action:** remember there are always things you can do to change the situation you find yourself in. You can write down an action plan, attend a networking event, or start a new job application. You can choose to switch the narrative if you shift your attention to what you can control.
>
> **5. Seek help and talk it out:** if you reach a point where you feel your mental health or wellbeing is being affected by your job search, you should talk to someone about it. Whether this is a friend, a family member, or a professional, don't suffer alone.

Interviews & Assessment Centres

Once you have reached the interview stage of a recruitment process, the role or internship is yours for the taking. You've clearly met the firm's initial requirements in terms of academic performance, prior experience, motivation and the like. However, now you will need to support the assertions made in your application, evidence your communication skills and demonstrate in greater detail how you have acquired a foundation of the key skills, strengths and knowledge required to succeed in the role. This section focuses on how to prepare for interview and assessment centres.

What do assessment centres typically involve?

Ice breakers

"Ice breaker" activities are fairly common at the start of assessment centres, especially if you'll be interacting with other candidates. Ice breakers can range from firm to firm, but they usually involve each candidate introducing themselves to the others. I have also participated in ice breakers where we have each been asked to state two truths and a lie (so that the other candidates can then work together to try to figure out the lie), or to tell the others an interesting fact about ourselves or give an insight into what we do for fun. It's never something particularly tricky, as the main aim is to help you relax into the day. From what I know, these exercises aren't generally assessed, so don't let them compound the stress you'll likely already be feeling. Either way, just be yourself and get stuck in. This can reflect positively on your social skills and confidence, plus if you happen to have a particularly interesting fact to mention if asked, why not shed some positive light on yourself at the start!. Also use these exercises to try to remember people's names, as this can help you to build a rapport with others at the get-go (which might be especially useful if you later have to work in a group with them).

Competency, motivation and commercial awareness questions

There are four key elements that firms tend to focus on when setting application questions and interviewing candidates, so try to bear these in mind whilst preparing for interviews and assessment centres (we cover each element in more detail later):

- **Career motivation:** firms will want to understand your motivation for pursuing your career of choice, so you will need to reflect on how your experiences have influenced your decision to pursue your desired career. In other words, you need to persuade the firm that you actually want to do the job (e.g. be a lawyer) and more particularly, do the job at that type of firm (e.g. a City, regional or boutique firm).

- **Firm motivation:** firms will want to know your reasons for wanting to work for them. Research the firms you are applying to/interviewing at so that you are able to differentiate them from their competitors and explain why these differentiating factors particularly appeal to you. In other words, you need to persuade the firm you want to do the job *there*.

- **Competencies, strengths and experiences:** firms will want to gain an insight into the skills and capabilities you have developed through your studies, extracurricular activities and work experience. In other words, you need to persuade the firm that you're good enough for the role. Before an assessment centre, remind yourself of your work experiences, positions of responsibility and extracurricular involvements, including the skills and abilities you developed through each.

- **Commercial awareness:** firms may want to see evidence of your interest in and understanding of current affairs and the industry you are looking to work in, as this can reflect on your interest in the work the firm carries out, as well as your commercial acumen (which can be key to success in the role). To test your commercial awareness, you might be asked to discuss a recent commercial news story or comment more generally on the industry trends that affect the firm and its clients. As part of a commercial assessment, you may also have to complete commercial case studies or tackle interviews that require you to discuss, for example, key business concepts, commercial risks and opportunities, different options for financing deals, mergers and acquisitions and more. You may also have to explain the role of the firm/different departments when advising clients in different contexts.

Presentations

When candidates are asked to prepare a presentation for an interview, they tend to really panic about the content. However, presentations aren't usually about demonstrating everything you know. If you try to cram in too much information, or you deliver content that is overly complex or technical, you could be setting yourself up to fail. A presentation exercise is usually designed to test your communication skills. Your ability to discuss a topic in a succinct, easily digestible and engaging manner. The topic itself is less important; it's more about how you structure the presentation, deliver the content and connect with your interviewer. Structure is key, as without a strong structure, it might be difficult to follow what you're saying. Speak at a steady pace, maintain eye contact (or look at the webcam, if delivering the presentation virtually), and make sure you are maintaining positive, open body language. And smile from time to time! We cover how to deliver effective presentations in more detail below.

Group exercises

Most employers seek to hire strong team players who are eager to contribute, and able to listen to and encourage others. And for this reason, many assessment centres include some form of group exercise to test the way in which candidates interact with others on a mutual task (and sometimes also to test candidates' commercial awareness and knowledge of the firm). Assessment centre group exercises could involve a whole host of scenarios. including: completing a creative task in a group, for instance building a Lego tower in line with specific instructions; engaging in fictitious commercial negotiations, sometimes with more than two opposing sides; or discussing various commercial courses of action as a group before agreeing which one to pursue.

Throughout team-based assessments, constantly keep in mind that you're primarily being tested on your ability to work cohesively, communicate effectively, and build a positive rapport with others (i.e. which includes your social skills and emotional intelligence). Although your performance during a group exercise might not, in isolation, secure you the role, it can definitely cause you to miss out. And graduate recruiters are very perceptive, so are likely to notice if the attitude of one or two candidates adversely impacts upon the team dynamic (even if this dynamic only tends to surface when candidates are working together in private).

Be polite, courteous and supportive throughout, not obnoxious, competitive, overbearing or argumentative. After all, these exercises are about collaboration, not competition. Candidates who are outwardly competitive are not generally looked upon favourably, as this can indicate they would negatively impact the firm's culture if they were to be offered a job. Moreover, don't use group exercises as an excuse to show off everything you know for the sake of it. This will annoy others in the group, and might be seen as you failing to give others the chance to contribute. On that note, don't speak over people or be overly dismissive of their ideas. Instead, consider asking others for their opinions, and perhaps try to encourage quieter team members to speak. Asking people what *they* think (rather than just telling everyone what *you* think) is a quick and simple way of demonstrating that you value the opinions of others and can therefore work effectively in a team.

Make sure you're then receptive of any ideas that come to light, and be prepared to concede. Or at least deal constructively and delicately with ideas that you believe are somewhat irrelevant or objectively wrong. One way of showing that you're a strong team player is to credit others' contributions, draw together ideas that have been raised, then suggest a way of moving forward.

Practical tips: at the start of a group exercise, consider proposing a plan to follow for the session to ensure the group meets any objectives it has been set. Doing so means you will have contributed at the outset, which can take the pressure off a little and let you bide your time and properly think through the task before contributing again. You could also offer to keep time, but if you do, make sure you get it right, and avoid getting distracted by the clock. In addition, try to use people's names throughout. This can demonstrate that you're paying attention, whilst helping you to build a rapport with your teammates.

For more detailed advice on how to approach ice breakers, presentations and group exercises, check out:
www.commerciallaw.academy/courses/interviews
www.commerciallaw.academy/courses/presentations

Market-sizing and brainteaser questions

Certain assessment centres, especially in the context of investment banking or consulting, may require you to tackle "market sizing" questions or "brainteasers". These are designed to assess the thought process you follow and logic you apply when tackling a challenging problem, and test how well you react to unexpected questions under pressure.

Q. How many footballs could fill up Wembley Stadium?

Q. How much milk does Starbucks use on a typical working day in the UK?

Q. How many shoes are sold in India every year?

Q. How many cars are there on average in the UK at any given time?

When answering these types of questions, you are not generally expected to reach a final numerical answer that is particularly close to the true value. However, you will be expected to advance reasonable/rational assumptions and estimations along the way. It's therefore essential that you think out loud so the interviewer can follow your thought process. One way to approach market sizing questions is to break the question down into little problems and then consider (out loud) all the possible variables that could affect the answer. For example, If you are asked how many cars are sold by BMW in the UK every year, does this mean only cars branded with the BMW logo, or cars produced by BMW (for instance, Minis)? Does this only include new cars, or the sale of second hand BMWs? Do you include cars sold by UK dealerships to purchasers in other countries? You should also try to strike a balance between pragmatism and accuracy throughout, for example by rounding up numbers and working with averages when necessary (just to ensure that you can make calculations mentally if required). We cover brainteasers in more detail, including worked examples, in our *Consultancy Handbook*.

Preparing for interviews and assessment centres

As a general caveat to the content in this section, try to avoid *over* preparing. During interviews, it is essential that you answer the *specific questions* you are asked, not the questions that you happened to prepare for in advance and hoped to be asked. Interview questions can come in many different forms, with subtle nuances that require slightly different types of answers, so know your experiences and motivations well enough (and ensure you've built sufficiently solid commercial awareness) to enable you to adapt your answers accordingly. With this in mind, I'll now provide some preparation tips that personally helped when preparing for and attending interviews.

Compiling your notes

Treat interviews a little like exams. The more work you put in to accumulate the knowledge on which you might be assessed, the less likely it is that you will face a question that you do not know how to answer. When preparing for interviews, I created separate documents covering each distinct element on which I would likely be assessed: competencies, strengths and experiences; firm motivation; career motivation; current affairs; and commercial knowledge. In fact, the "commercial knowledge" document laid the foundations for what eventually became my Commercial Law Handbook. As sad as it sounds, I would then sit in a café on the morning of each of my interviews and highlight the key takeaways in each of the documents, much like revising for an exam.

The competencies, strengths and experiences document would set out my key experiences, the skills I had developed as a result of these experiences, and which experiences I would draw upon first for each type of competency question. For example, I had pre-decided that if "teamworking" came up, I would first talk about a specific university group project, whereas if "leadership" came up, I would first talk about running a university society. I made sure I also had a second option to hand for each of the more common competency questions, just in case firms asked multiple questions around a single competency (this actually happened on multiple occasions). This document also included a version of my CV with much more detail about my experiences written out in footnotes (more on this in the *Competencies, Strengths & Experience* chapter), plus a hard copy of my online application (so I could review the information I had already sent the firm, and try to anticipate questions that might consequently come my way).

> **Practical tip**
>
> Once you've decided which competencies and strengths you will prepare for, think about which of your experiences will best demonstrate each. Helpful preparation can include listing out these skills and strengths (perhaps as headings on a page), then noting down multiple experiences that you could draw upon to demonstrate each (perhaps underneath each heading). I did this, and ranked each experience so that I knew which I would want to draw upon first if asked about a particular competency. And this saved me, as in some interviews, I was asked multiple questions about my experience of utilising one particular skill.
>
> Alternatively, you could first list out all the interesting and relevant experiences that you have accumulated – again, as headings on a page – then note down each of the skills and strengths that you could demonstrate through each experience (this can also help to stimulate proper reflection on your experiences).
>
> Whichever approach you take, structuring your thoughts in this way can help you to avoid repeatedly relying on the same experience during an interview (which, as mentioned, you should avoid if you want to come across as well-rounded). And when completing this exercise, remember to consider not just relevant work experience, but also your positions of responsibility, society and sports team roles, group projects, casual part-time jobs, and so on.

On the day

This should go without saying, but on the day of your interview, be sure to arrive at least half an hour before your interview is due to start. If the firm's office is spread across different buildings, or has multiple entrances (which many do), make sure you know precisely where you need to be (and leave enough time to visit multiple locations in case you get it wrong). If you're travelling to London from elsewhere in the country, make sure there are at least a couple of back up trains that can still get you to the interview on time if your first train is cancelled (or you miss it). Plus, the earlier you arrive, the more time you can spend in a nearby café reading over your notes and calming your nerves.

Finally, remember that your interview starts from the moment you walk into the building. All too often interviewees are so consumed by nerves that they forget to act normally and be nice! The way you talk to reception staff and other interviewees in the waiting area may all form part of the test, so don't let your nerves mask your approachability and social skills.

> **Practical tip:** when attending interviews, I always carried pens, paper, coloured tabs and highlighters on me. The pens and paper meant that I could take notes after each of my interviews, whilst the tabs and highlighters were a life saver during the preparation phase prior to case study interviews. You could also consider bringing along anything else that might help you to support your answers to interview questions (although seek permission before rifling through your bag to find something). For example, I was once asked to explain how I prioritise my time, and ended up showing the interviewer a copy of my calendar and task list.

Your verbal and non-verbal communication

Throughout interviews, as well as your competencies and motivations, firms will likely also be assessing your composure, confidence, communication skills, interpersonal skills and enthusiasm. After all, your interviewer will need to know that you're able to act calmly and professionally if introduced to a client. Pay attention to what you say (i.e. your words), how you say it (i.e. your pace and expression), and how you look when you say it (i.e. your body language and eye contact). This is important, as what you say might lack credibility if you look or sound like you don't believe in what you're saying. With this in mind, below are some tips on how to improve your interview technique.

What you say and how you say it

How to stop rambling

Many people tend to ramble when they're nervous, me included! However, in interviews, you need to try to be concise and adopt a clear structure throughout your answers. There's only so much you can do in advance to avoid going off on a tangent. But if you actively keep this concern in the forefront of your mind, you'll hopefully become more self-aware, and therefore more likely to notice if you're deviating from the question.

Practical tip: if you do feel that you're going off on a tangent or speaking too much, try to recalibrate. One technique that has helped my mentees in the past is stopping to ask something to the effect of "would you like me to elaborate on anything I've just said?". Doing so temporarily deflected the focus from them, which gave them a moment to calm down, collect their thoughts and recalibrate. Alternatively, you could perhaps ask the interviewer a question relating to what you've been discussing. Again, this will give you a moment to collect your thoughts, and might also help to demonstrate your natural curiosity and interest in the subject matter you're discussing.

Pace and projection

Speaking in a clear, audible voice and taking the time to properly articulate words can make you easier to understand. This will enable the interviewer to gain more from your communication, which can consequently reflect more positively on your knowledge and capabilities. You should also always strive to speak at a reasonable pace so that people can properly understand you and digest what you are saying. This is especially important when speaking English, as the language is consonant-driven, meaning it is harder to understand when spoken too quickly. On a similar note, if your interviewers are taking notes, consider pausing from time to time, as they'll likely struggle to take in everything you're saying whilst simultaneously writing notes.

Practical tip: people often speak more quickly than they realise they do, especially when nervous or excited. With this in mind, perhaps record yourself answering mock interview questions in advance to check your pace, then listen back, adjust your pace if necessary, and repeat the process until you become more familiar with how the "right" pace feels. What feels unnaturally slow to you might sound perfect when you're listening back to a recording. And if you notice your pace increasing during an interview, don't be afraid to take a sip of water to help you reset.

Body language

During an interview, it's important that you consistently convey enthusiasm, as this will add credibility to your answers to motivation questions and indicate that you will fit nicely into the firm's culture. Positive, open body language is also key, as this can convey confidence, that you believe in what you are saying, and that you care about the conversation topics, which in turn can make you more engaging, help you to build a rapport, and reinforce the notion that you are genuinely happy to be there and interested in the role. So remain aware of your body language, and consciously adapt it when necessary.

In addition, try to avoid nervous ticks. Saying "um" too frequently, foot tapping, swaying, elaborate hand gestures (i.e. visual noise), standing on one leg and so on can all distract your audience. Consciously holding your hands together loosely at the start of the interview could help you to avoid some of these ticks. However, the best way to identify and mitigate ticks (of which you may well be unaware) is to practise in front of a friend and seek feedback, or to film yourself and watch it back. Most ticks can be avoided – or at least mitigated – through self-awareness and practice.

Finally, try to make great eye contact with your interviewer(s) throughout the interview, and if you have multiple interviewers, be democratic with that eye contact (i.e. make an effort to look at each of the interviewers roughly equally throughout). Also, look at them for a second (rather than a split second) to really achieve *engagement*. In my experience, eye contact tends to be one of the first things to go when people feel nervous, so consciously fight the urge to look away for long periods when you feel under pressure.

Composure

Interviews are nerve racking experiences. Many of us naturally revert into the age old "fight or flight" mentality, which can emerge when we're experiencing an "unknown" such as an interview with people we've never met. Try to recognise and accept that this is a natural physiological response – remembering that the vast majority of candidates will be equally as nervous (if not more) – then do your best to counter the symptoms of stress. Try to keep calm, take deep breaths and don't be afraid to ask for thinking time or clarification.

Practical tip: if you are offered a glass of water at the start of an interview, say yes! When nervous, I tend to become overly polite, which has led to me declining a glass of water at the outset of interviews in the past (purely as a knee jerk reaction). However, taking a sip of water can enable you to pause, calm your nerves, and take a second to think through your responses before speaking out loud. It's about buying yourself some time while you wait for inspiration to strike. In addition, without water, your nerves and constant talking can lead to your mouth becoming really dry (which can sound strange), so just say "yes"!

You may also be specifically tested on your composure during an interview. In one interview, I was asked who I would choose to have dinner if I could invite anyone, living or dead. I certainly hadn't prepared for this question and it caught me of guard. But I then reminded myself that it was likely a test of composure, so I took a deep breath and said "Mick Jagger from the Rolling Stones". It wasn't a particularly intelligent answer, but I remained composed and justified this on the basis that one evening with Mick would give me enough stories to entertain clients for the rest of my career. And I got the internship offer. It just goes to show that sometimes it's less about the answer, and more about how you handle the situation.

I was also once asked by one firm to pitch one of their competitors, as my CV showed that I had been that competitor's campus ambassador. I took a deep breath and gave a deadpan pitch, drawing out all the positives of that competitor's business, then took some time to explain why my preference remained the interviewer's firm. My answer went down well and I received an internship offer; it would probably not have gone so well had I panicked, or tried to speak negatively of that competitor instead. On that note, never speak negatively about another firm. It's fine to draw out the elements that you prefer about a prospective employer, but if you slander one of their competitors, this could come across as unprofessional (and might lead your interviewer to assume that you're capable of being equally as negative about their firm in other situations).

You might also be challenged – sometimes quite strongly – on your responses in an interview. When this happens, try to keep calm and don't be afraid to disagree with your interviewers, as long as you're sure you're not objectively wrong and you can justify your comments! I was once asked whether I would ever accept a bribe. I said no (professional ethics are absolute!), but the interviewer kept testing whether my mind could be changed, making comments such as "but what if the client insists and it's the only way to get a deal over the line?". I stood my ground, as was praised in my feedback for doing so.

In another interview, I was asked whether I should drop some of my extra-curricular activities to increase my chances of securing a 1st class degree. Again, I said no, on the basis that the skills I have developed (and would continue to develop) as a result of my extra-curriculars were equally – if not more – valuable than gaining a 1st. The conversation continued for quite some time, but again, I stood my ground, and this didn't stop me securing an internship offer.

What if you can't think of a response to a question?

You've prepared properly for the interview, it's all going swimmingly and then along comes a tricky question ... suddenly your mind goes completely blank. It's happened to us all, but what you do next might determine whether it's game over, or whether you can prove your resilience and get a bit closer to that job offer. We asked ex-City lawyer and experienced Career Consultant Claire Leslie what you should do if you can't think of an answer during an interview. According to Claire, the first thing you need to do is to think about what kind of question you are facing. This will help you to determine how to respond.

A competency question

I once froze at interview when I was asked to talk about a time when I had worked with someone difficult. Now, I have, over the years, worked with plenty of difficult people, so why did I suddenly forget? Probably because I hadn't seen this coming – poor planning – and because what sprang into my mind was a negative experience. I did not want to talk about this at interview. It is never good to be negative about previous employments. I did the right thing, I asked to come back to the question later, but then I let it play on my mind while I answered successive questions. It distracted me and impacted my performance. Do ask to come back to a question, but don't then stop concentrating on everything else! As mentioned earlier in this handbook, taking the time in advance to list out and carefully consider all the experiences you have accumulated can help you to think up examples on the spot when unexpected questions come up.

A technical question

If your degree is relevant to the role for which you are applying, then you might find that you are asked technical questions. Try not to panic about questions you find difficult; the more anxious you are, the more likely it is that your mind will go blank. Take time to think. Employers will almost always be happy for you to pause; they would rather have an employee who reflects on difficult questions than one who rushes in and makes errors!

Remember that a pause while you think will feel much longer to you than it actually is. Also remember that employers may ask questions knowing that you will likely be unable to answer them. They may simply be looking to test: (a) how well you react under pressure; (b) how well you can apply logic on the spot to reach a reasonable conclusion; and (c) the point at which you no longer have an answer (i.e. where your knowledge ends)! You might have got a lot further than other candidates before you had to admit defeat, even though it may not feel like this at the time. Try not to feel deflated or let your disappointment at not answering everything play on your mind during the rest of the interview.

An oddball question

Oddball (i.e. unexpected and seemingly random) questions are often talked about and feared. How many bricks are there in Birmingham? How many pints of milk are drunk each day in the UK? You are not expected to know the answer to these questions, just try not to freeze completely. The important thing is how you start to think and reason your way to an answer. Demonstrate that you are logical and can keep calm under pressure and you are already on the road to success. The City Career Series Consultancy Handbook explains how to answer such "brainteaser" and "market-sizing" questions in more detail.

A strengths-based question

You would have thought that a question about how you spend your spare time or what you do to relax would be very simple. However, sometimes these questions can floor you. You may be trying to think of something which *you believe* sounds worthwhile and impressive, when actually in truth you like going shopping with friends! It's worth thinking about answers in advance (using the *Common strengths-based questions* section of this handbook for guidance), and ensuring that you have a really clear understanding of the skills for which an employer is looking. Ultimately, if the unexpected question comes up, you need to answer honestly. You're likely to get caught out in a strengths-based interview if you lie.

Asking questions

It's easy to forget this, but interviews are *two way* conversations between yourself and your interviewers. They provide a great opportunity for the firm to get to know you, but also offer you the chance to get to know a bit more about the firm and its people. You should always come armed with questions, as failing to ask questions if given the opportunity at the end of an interview might demonstrate a lack of interest in learning more about the firm (and therefore reflect negatively on your motivation and interest). It also means you will have wasted a unique opportunity to gain further insights into the firm and its culture.

Tailor your questions to the role and seniority of your interviewers. If you're talking to a senior partner or a director, don't start asking them about the application process. Consider asking them about their career: what has kept them at the firm for so long, how has their role changed over time, what is their favourite thing about the job etc. These types of questions can demonstrate your desire to gain a greater insight into the firm. You could also ask about the firm's future strategies, or how it negotiated a particular challenge, although be ready to give your own opinion in case they flip the question back onto you.

If you are being interviewed by a graduate recruiter, you could perhaps ask about the work that you might encounter on a vacation scheme, the nature of the training throughout the graduate scheme, or the opportunities you may have during the graduate scheme (ahead of any rotations) to learn about the work carried out by different teams.

You should also listen carefully to everything your interviews say, as this might help you to think of additional questions to ask at the end. In each of my interviews, the interviewers introduced themselves, briefly summarised their career paths to date, and provided an insight into their specialisms. I then tried to remember this information so that I could use it to form targeted questions to ask at the end. For example, asking how the firm's merger a few years back affected your interviewers when they were junior associates in the banking team shows a thoughtful and personal interest in the people sat in front of you.

Practical tip: remember your interviewers' names! Perhaps write them down when you leave the interview room. During assessment centres that involved multiple interviews, I was often asked in my second or third interview who had interviewed me previously, and I couldn't always remember.

Virtual interviews

Much of the advice that applies to in-person interviews also applies to "live" and video interviews, however here are some specific tips to help in the virtual domain.

What are virtual interviews?

Increasingly, before attending an in-person interview or assessment centre, candidates are having to attend some form of virtual interview. This could be a "live" virtual interview, meaning an interview with a human interviewer that takes place using video conferencing software such as Zoom, Skype, Microsoft Teams or Google Meet. Alternatively, it could be a "video" interview, which involves you having to record your answers to pre-determined questions and submit them through some form of portal.

Key insight from Hannah Salton: virtual interviews can enable firms to scale their assessment processes at a far lower cost, whilst ensuring that interviews are conducted consistently and without the level of bias that inevitably arises when relying on a large and diverse pool of internal interviewers.

During video interviews, you will typically face a series of pre-recorded questions. After each question pops up, you might be allocated a very limited period of time (sometimes only a minute) within which to formulate your answer, compose yourself, and then deliver the answer, so it's imperative that you're familiar with all the experiences that you can use as the basis for your answers.

Key insight from Hannah Salton: don't rush through your answer to try and squeeze more content in – the recruiter will be looking for detail and depth to what you say. Try and use all or most of the time you are given to respond, but avoid padding out your answer with fluff and buzzwords if you have said everything you have to say.

Video interviews can feel very unnatural, artificial and impersonal, as you don't have the opportunity to gauge and feed off human emotions and reactions. However, try to remember that all candidates are in the same boat and will likely be experiencing the same unease, so you won't necessarily be at a disadvantage in the grand scheme of things.

Key insight from Hannah Salton: you aren't expected to perform exactly the same as you would in a "normal" interview environment. The person watching your video back will have been trained specifically in how to assess video interview answers, and will understand the artificial context in which the interview has taken place.

If you are invited to a video interview, try to find out in advance which questions will be asked (or at least which competencies will be tested) and how long you will have to answer each. I wouldn't recommend writing out "model answers" in advance to read out (as this can come across as robotic and unengaging) and if you've spoken to other candidates about their experiences, don't assume that you'll be asked the same questions in the same order. Firms might mix it up.

Top tip from Hannah Salton: even though you're not in the same room as the person watching you, you need to think about body language. Sit up straight, use your hands naturally to support what you're saying, and try and show energy and enthusiasm. Be clear and concise, and practice out loud to ensure you are getting across your motivation and passion in a measured and natural way. You might want to record yourself and watch the footage back to reflect on how you come across. This can feel quite embarrassing, but it can be really helpful for increasing your self-awareness!

How should you prepare?

Before commencing a video interview, familiarise yourself with the relevant platform, including reviewing any instructional videos and other guidance if necessary. Connect early in case you experience any technical difficulties and make sure you check that the camera is on and you're not on mute. Dress as you would for a "normal" interview, and not just your top half! In a "live" interview, you never know for sure whether you'll need to get up for some reason, perhaps to go and grab something in support of one of your answers, or to get a glass of water.

Make sure you are in a quiet, private, well-lit room and that your background is respectable and clutter free. A chaotic background might suggest that *you* are a little chaotic. Empty rooms might create an echo however, so ideally use a room with a carpet or items that will reduce reverberations.

Where possible, shut out pets and make sure everyone else in the house is aware that you are interviewing so that they don't disturb you. Disturbances can really disrupt your flow of thought and also come across as unprofessional. Saying that, I have had various people (including my son) barge into the room during client calls and live webinars, so I fully appreciate that this isn't always possible, and firms will likely be understanding in these circumstances. However, you have nothing to lose by doing what you can to mitigate the risk of disruption.

Try to ensure that you have a strong internet connection by sitting as close to the router as possible and ensuring that you (and any cohabitants) aren't streaming music or videos at the same time. Also make sure your browsers, email clients and messaging apps are closed, otherwise you (and your interviewers!) might be distracted by notifications, and make sure that your phone is *off* (not only on silent), just in case your phone is connected to your laptop and a phone call rings through your laptop speakers.

If there's even the slightest chance you will need to screen share, make sure your desktop is clear, your background photo is appropriate, and no other documents or programmes are open. I once left my browser open and my phone on whilst delivering a live webinar. During the webinar, I received 100+ LinkedIn notifications from attendees (which was highly distracting) and then had a call from my mother ring through my laptop speakers. Not ideal!

Consider using headphones (if they have an in-built microphone), as they might offer a better quality of sound, whilst also helping to block out any potentially distracting external noise. Try to avoid typing, as this might give the interviewer the impression that you are Googling answers. If you want to take notes, use a good old fashioned pen and paper.

And finally, don't forget that the webcam lens is your equivalent of eye contact. Make sure it is roughly eye level and focus on this as much as possible, as doing so will help you to build a connection with – and therefore engage – your listener. It's easy to get distracted by the videos of yourself and your interviewer on the screen, so make a conscious effort not to.

> **Practical tip:** one tip that has worked well for students I have coached involves sticking a post-it note next to your webcam, and drawing an arrow towards the camera lens to constantly remind you to stare at it. If you tend to speak too fast, you could also write "SLOW' on the post-it note, and if you don't naturally smile in interview situations, perhaps add a smiley face too. This can all help you to recalibrate when slipping into bad presenting habits during an interview (or virtual meeting, for that matter).

Preparing for interviews and assessment centres

📄 24 lessons
▶ 1 hour of video content

Negotiation

📄 8 lessons

Delivering effective presentations and managing nerves

📄 18 lessons
▶ 1 hour of video content

CVs, Cover Letters & LinkedIn Profiles

I'll start by acknowledging that there is no objectively "correct" way to approach CVs, cover letters and LinkedIn profiles. Different firms in different industries will have different preferences, so it's always worth carrying out a little research to ascertain the basics of what firms expect (for example, one page or two, school grades or only university grades, and so on). With this in mind, this chapter provides some basic pointers that you may want to consider.

CVs

Bear in mind that whilst a majority of financial services firms tend to expect one-page CVs, some – especially law firms – prefer two-page CVs. On the flip side, some firms do not request CVs at all. Before starting to draft your CV, check whether the firm you're applying to has any specific requirements, and perhaps see if anyone in your network has an example of a CV that has previously helped an applicant to secure an interview there. Now, we all know that CVs provide an insight into your past experiences and achievements, but don't forget that they also evidence your writing style, your ability to distil information into short, concise sentences, your skill at structuring documents, and your attention to detail.

To that end, avoid spelling and grammatical mistakes, ensure the fonts and text sizes you use are consistent, and check that dates and bullet points are in a coherent format and properly aligned (e.g. if using a hyphen to indicate date ranges such as Feb 2022 – July 2023, use identical hyphens and consistent spacing either side of those hyphens throughout. People almost always get this wrong!). In this context, it can really help to ask others to proofread your CV, as they may be able to offer a fresh perspective. In addition, your layout should look professional: avoid the use of flowery borders, bright colours and cartoon images (it happens!) and make sure the structure clearly outlines your experiences and achievements, *even on a quick skim*. This is important, as recruiters are unlikely to pour over your CV for long; there's evidence to suggest many take no longer than 30 seconds!

To achieve structural clarity, you could split your CV into sections, as I have done in the adjacent example. Note that by splitting out "Relevant" and "Other" work experience, you can prioritise your most relevant work experience, whilst still maintaining a chronological order within each section (this can be helpful if, for example, you have carried out a less relevant role more recently than a relevant role).

Once you have your sections, then make sure that the names of organisations and your various roles can be easily identified on a skim read (i.e. make them stand out). In other words, try to make recruiters' lives easier.

On a separate note, keep your sentences concise and to the point and avoid repetition, but don't be afraid to include more interesting or unique interests and experiences if you have space, as this can help you to stand out. Whatever you include, use the space on the page wisely. Bullet points that contain only a couple of words could suggest you have little to say about yourself.

Finally, and this is something that people often get wrong: give proper context when discussing your experiences. Don't assume that the reader will inherently understand what the organisations you mention do, or what your role involved. Giving proper context about what you have done can help to legitimately evidence the skills that you developed and utilised.

When discussing your experience, it is generally considered good practice to avoid using personal pronouns such as "I" and "we", as this can read more professionally. For example, you could start a bullet point with "Reviewed documents…" rather than "*I* reviewed documents…". Other helpful phrases include "Role involved…", "Responsibilities included…", "Completed…", "Tasked with…" etc.

Personal Details
Name, address, phone number, email address, LinkedIn

Education
Include your secondary school and university (plus at least university grades), and relevant qualifications

Relevant Work Experience
Include experience that directly relates to the role you're applying for, including part-time roles and internships

Other Work Experience
Include other paid and unpaid work experience, for example casual part-time summer jobs

Positions Of Responsibility
Include non-work experiences where you had a substantive role (e.g. society roles, team captaincies, volunteering, mentoring)

Extracurricular Activities
Include activities where you participated, but didn't have much responsibility (e.g. being in a sports team or music ensemble)

Additional Skills, Interests & Awards
Include anything else that might reflect well on you (e.g. scholarships, prizes, certifications, music grades, hobbies)

Cover letters

As with CVs, there is no objectively correct way to structure cover letters. Some firms may set word or character limits, whilst others may simply ask you to attach a separate document. Cover letters for certain roles may also require a different emphasis. A speculative application for casual work experience can call for a very different technique than that required when making full-time job applications. For example, if you are applying for experience at a small high street firm, you will not necessarily need to spend ages distinguishing it from its competitors. However, do try to approach cover letters in this context with a focus on "what I can do for you" rather than "what you can do for me". With all this in mind, before getting started, there's no harm in doing a little research to gauge what is expected from you.

Either way, cover letters should be fairly concise – usually no longer than a page – and well written, with a strong structure. After all, this may well provide the firm with its first impression of the standard of work that you're able to deliver. To that end, using temporary headings whilst drafting your cover letter can help you to maintain a clear structure from the outset.

A cover letter for an established graduate scheme at a large City firm should probably include an overview of your reasons for making the application and an insight into why you believe you are a suitable candidate. The structure I usually go for involves kicking off with an introductory sentence explaining where I'm currently at (e.g. "I am a penultimate year Law & Business student at Warwick University"), as well as mentioning the specific role or placement that I'm applying for (e.g. "I am applying for the [Firm Name] 2023 summer vacation scheme". I'll then cover why I'm interested in the career, why I'm interested in the firm, and why I think I'd succeed in the role, before finishing off with a conclusion, which might thank them in advance for considering my application. Rather than using headings in my final draft, I'll make sure my introductory sentence for each main paragraph clearly sign posts what I'm talking about. For example:

- My career motivation paragraph might start with "My interest in commercial law stems from…"

- My firm motivation paragraph might then start with "I am applying to [Firm Name] in particular for the following key reasons…"

- My "Why you" paragraph might kick off with "Finally, I believe I have developed a foundation of the competencies required to succeed as a trainee solicitor…".

Your Details

Firm Details

Date

1. **Salutation (Dear…)**

   Try to find the name of the specific person that will be receiving your application. This shows good research and professionalism. Otherwise, use "Dear Sir/Madam".

2. **Heading**

   Summarise the main purpose of the letter using a bold heading between the salutation and the introduction, e.g. **'2023 Summer Internship Application'**.

3. **Introduction**

   Explain where you're currently at and mention the role/opportunity for which you are applying (e.g. I am a penultimate year Law & Business student at Warwick University, and I am writing to apply for the [Firm Name] 2023 summer vacation scheme").

4. **State your reasons for applying for the job**

   Tell the story of how your interest in your chosen career has developed (see the *Career Motivation* section of this handbook for help with this step).

5. **State your reasons for applying to the particular firm**

   Think of legitimate ways to differentiate the firm and more importantly, relate these elements back to *you* in order to convince recruiters that these factors genuinely appeal (see the *Firm Motivation* section of this handbook for help with this step).

6. **Explain why you believe that you are a suitable candidate**

   Draw on your experiences to highlight your skills and strengths, then relate these to the competencies required for the role in question (see the *Competencies, Strengths & Experience* section of this handbook for help with this step).

7. **Conclusion**

   You could thank the reader for considering your application, then sign off. Sign off with "Yours sincerely" if you know the name of the reader, or 'Yours faithfully' if you don't.

Your LinkedIn profile

People have written entire books on LinkedIn, so there's clearly a huge amount of advice to bear in mind. However, for the purposes of this handbook, we'll keep it short and to the point. To summarise, your LinkedIn profile should reflect what you've previously done, what you're currently doing, what you're good at, and what you're looking for. It should highlight all your relevant experiences and draw out your key skills and achievements. And it should always be up-to-date. Just like a CV.

It's essential to keep in mind is that your LinkedIn profile is public and accessible 24/7 from all over the world. In that sense, having a LinkedIn profile is a little like sending out your CV to everyone in your network – and everyone outside of your network – every second of every day. It's also becoming increasingly common for interviewers to have a quick skim of a candidate's LinkedIn profile before an interview and for supervisors to have a cheeky skim before you start an internship or graduate role. With this in mind, ask yourself the following: would you send your CV to everyone you know – plus future interviewers and supervisors – without first ensuring it's up-to-date, it's accurate and it positively reflects your abilities and experiences? The right answer, of course, is "no", but many people don't think about LinkedIn in the same way. However they (and you) really should.

The first impression

Remember, for people you haven't met before, your LinkedIn profile may well provide their first impression of you. So, for starters, make sure that your profile is well-written and free from spelling and grammatical errors – you may be judged on your writing style as much as the quality of your prior endeavours – and ensure that your photograph is recent and professional (no photos from Ayia Napa 2019, this isn't Facebook!). Moreover, your LinkedIn profile headline should succinctly capture what you're currently doing and, if you're a student, what you're currently looking for (e.g. "Second year Chemistry student looking for investment banking opportunities"). Then as you progress in your career, you might shift the focus to outline your particular specialism (e.g. "I'm a management consultant with a focus on the technology sector"). On a related note, most recruiters use LinkedIn these days when headhunting candidates, and your headline (and job title) will often determine whether you appear in those recruiters' search results when they are trying to find potential candidates to fulfil certain roles. This can be particularly important later in your career if you start to consider switching firms or roles.

Skills and experiences

You should get in the habit of adding to your LinkedIn profile every new experience that you complete, as soon as you complete it. If you have attended a virtual internship or an office visit, stick it on there, including the firm's name, what you did, and what you got out of it. Also include your positions of responsibility (including roles on university society executive committees), and feel free to throw in a few interests and extracurricular activities to show that you're a well-rounded individual. Also make sure you give proper context about the organisations you have worked for and the nature of your role. Don't assume others will inherently understand this stuff.

Media and hyperlinks

Consider publishing content to show off your knowledge, expertise and interests. The initiative and drive that this requires might impress recruiters and interviewers, plus the content itself could help you to attract the attention of potential contributors, mentors and employers. More specifically, adding photos or hyperlinks can help to support the statements you make. For example, if you talk about your public speaking experience, why not evidence it with a photo of you speaking in front of a crowd. If you talk about your creative skills, perhaps share a link to (or upload) a portfolio of your work. If you write blogs or commercial awareness updates, link to some of your writing examples. This can all help to add some credibility and authenticity to your profile, whilst also enabling you to stand out.

Publishing and engaging with content

Posting on LinkedIn can help to inform others about your skills, strengths and experiences, and alert them to anything in particular that you're seeking. This in turn might improve your chances of someone else recommending you for a particular role, or notifying you of potentially relevant opportunities that they have come across. To give a personal example, when I first started working as a copywriter for tech start-ups, I was mandated on a variety of interesting projects by people who had discovered me via my posts on LinkedIn and other social channels.

You could post about your successes (e.g. receiving an award), what you're up to (e.g. attending webinars or launching an enterprise), what you're offering (e.g. volunteering to write articles or carry out work experience relevant to the career you're pursuing), and the like. Or you could post key takeaways from the events, webinars or workshops you have attended, which your network might find helpful (and those who delivered the events may appreciate – I certainly do!). Then, to encourage engagement with your posts, share them with groups, use hashtags, and tag other people and organisations. You can also engage with others' posts by liking and sharing them, leaving comments, and asking them questions, which may lead to them returning the favour when you post! This can all also show that you use your initiative, you're pro-active and a self-starter, you're engaged, you're constantly looking to learn and progress, and you're genuinely interested in a particular topic or industry.

Competencies, Strengths & Experience

The recruitment process for City careers can involve an application stage, psychometric testing, a phone or Skype/video interview, and an assessment centre at the firm's offices (which might include, for example, a group exercise, presentation, written exercise, case study, and motivation/competency interview). These stages are predominantly designed to help a firm learn more about your strengths, capabilities and suitability to the role for which you are applying. In this chapter, we cover the key types of competency and strengths-based questions that you'll likely come across, including why they are relevant and how to approach them. We then include advice from a careers adviser in connection with some of the trickier questions that may come your way.

Drawing skills and strengths from your experiences

Firms may ask for examples of when you have demonstrated or acquired specific skills or strengths. They may ask about particular experiences or challenges you've faced. Or they may try to assess your skill development through evaluating your contribution or reaction in different scenarios (e.g. "when have you successfully led a team through a difficult situation?"). You may also face ethical questions, such as "would you ever pay a ransom?" (this came up for me) or "have you ever done anything ethically questionable?". Or you may be asked more open ended questions to assess your character and thought process, such as "when have you failed at something?", "what motivates you?" or "why did you choose your degree?". Questions can also be quite specific at times. For example, I was once asked to talk about a time when I had worked in a team and had to deal with a colleague that was not pulling their weight.

Ultimately, they will want to know why your interests, experiences, competencies and strengths make you an ideal candidate. So it's important that you properly consider all the experiences you have accumulated, and thoroughly reflect on how these have helped you to develop the skills, attributes and mindset sought by the firms to which you are applying. Ideally you should do this well in advance of writing applications and preparing for interviews. After all, the more experiences and competencies you have in the forefront of your mind, the better prepared you'll be to write compelling applications and deal with specific or unexpected questions during interviews.

Your experiences

Perhaps start by listing out *all* the experiences you have accumulated to date, as having these in the forefront of your mind can be useful when deciding which experiences you can use to evidence the skills, strengths and attributes you are asked about.

Which experiences are relevant?

It's good to draw upon a wide range of different experiences in your applications and interviews, both academic and non-academic, as this can help to demonstrate that you are a well-rounded individual. Remember that *any* of your experiences can be relevant to draw upon, no matter how trivial or irrelevant they might initially seem. Pretty much *any* experience – if discussed in the right away – should enable you to demonstrate at least a few key skills and positive character traits, regardless of whether it involved spending weeks in a large corporate office, contributing to a small family business, working a casual part-time job, or volunteering.

On that note, your experiences don't have to directly reflect the role you're applying for; they may instead provide useful reference points to demonstrate that you've developed important transferable skills or demonstrated positive character traits. Travelling, sport, music, volunteering, part-time work, debating, society roles, group work, tutoring, campus ambassador roles: all these experiences require specific skills and can demonstrate a broad range of attributes, including work ethic, commitment, motivation, interpersonal skills, professionalism, team-working and so on.

I have worked in catering, on a building site, in a supermarket, as a tutor, as a bin collector and as a paperboy. Discussing these experiences in my interviews actually helped me to find common ground with some of my interviews (who had worked similar jobs when they were younger). Plus they demonstrated work ethic, organisational skills, an ability to interact professionally with customers, and a broad range of other skills. On that note, any experience working in a service role – for example, working in a bar, in a retail store or on the checkouts of a supermarket – can also help to demonstrate that you've developed "client-facing" skills (as "client" is synonymous with "customer") and the ability to act professionally when representing a business.

Getting into the detail

As part of your interview preparation, ensure that you know exactly what you wrote in your application and be prepared to talk at length about any of the experiences you have mentioned. To that end, consider noting down as much detail as possible about each experience well in advance of interviews. This could include statistics to support your statements, for example: the number of tickets you sold for a ball, the percentage increase in sponsorship revenue that you helped to generate, or the number of members you managed to sign up to your society.

Practical tip: I used to keep a version of my CV in which every experience had a corresponding footnote. In each footnote, I would write down the details that didn't make it onto the main version of my CV, for example: the names of the people/teams I worked with; which presentations I attended and the topics that were covered; what my role involved on a day-to-day basis, and details of any tasks I completed; and anything else that might be relevant at a later stage. I would then study this on the morning of interviews to ensure that the detail was at the forefront of my mind.

To give a few examples of how various experiences might – if thought about in sufficient detail – have encompassed a broad range of responsibilities and challenges:

- If you are captain of your university's netball team, your role might involve securing sponsorship, negotiating the price of the team's kit, arranging training sessions, collaborating with other netball teams to arrange matches, organising transport for competitions, and motivating teammates.

- If you worked on a particularly challenging group project, this might have involved in-depth research, drafting a comprehensive report or pitch, working closely with other group members to pursue a common goal, working under pressure towards a strict deadline, and thinking creatively about the structure and presentation of your work.

- As mentioned earlier, if you have tutored younger students, this will likely have required you to interact professionally with them (and perhaps their parents), keep them motivated and engaged, communicate complex concepts in an easily digestible manner, organise and plan your lessons, adhere to strict deadlines, and adapt your approach to support tutees with differing abilities, of different ages, from different backgrounds and cultures, and so on.

- If you have been involved in debating or mooting, this will likely have involved public speaking, carrying out in-depth research, negotiating with others or trying to persuade them to accept your point of view, working closely in a team, and commitment.

- If you have been tasked with arranging a large event (such as a university ball), this will likely have involved conceptualising the event, setting ticket prices and raising funding, branding and marketing the event, managing the budget, negotiating with suppliers, coordinating a team of assistants, and running the event. Similar roles to those involved in running a business!

- If you have run a society, this might have involved: creating an innovative sponsorship pitch, securing funding (e.g. grants/firm sponsorship), negotiating sponsorship and prices (e.g. the cost of venues or branded merch), forming strategic partnerships, leading a team, recruiting and training junior exec members, establishing clear communication channels (e.g. through arranging regular meetings or setting up a team Slack channel), building a member base (e.g. through marketing, engaging with prospective members, and pitching at freshers' fairs), running events, and shaping/executing the society's broader strategy.

If you haven't taken the time to really think through your experiences in advance of an interview, you might forget many of these details whilst nervous or under pressure.

Your skills and strengths

Once you have noted all the details around your experiences, you should then take the time to really consider all the possible skills, competencies and strengths that you have developed as a result of the experiences you have accumulated. Here are some examples of the key skills that you might want to consider:

To prepare, research into the key skills and strengths that each firm is looking for – including each firm's specific explanation of what they mean by each skill and strength, as this can differ – then try to cover most (or all) of these in your answers. In addition, try to meet with people who have already been through the interview process at the firms you are applying to. They may be able to provide an insight into the types of questions that the firms may ask, or introduce you to someone who can. You can also attempt to research the types of question that firms have previously asked candidates online (although don't assume your interview questions will be identical to those faced by others).

Firms generally emphasise the skills that they most value during campus presentations and office visits, and on their websites. Although many firms highlight similar skills, some firms may place greater emphasis on one or two particular skills or values. Different firms (and even different interviewers within the same firm) take very different approaches to competency interviews, so be prepared to adapt your answers.

Finally, as mentioned earlier, it is essential that you answer the *specific question* you are being asked, not the question that you happened to prepare for in advance and hoped to be asked. Competency questions can come in many different forms, with subtle nuances that require slightly different types of answers, so know your experiences well enough to enable you to adapt your answers accordingly. This is where over preparation (such as trying to script answers in advance) can be a real hindrance!

Structuring your answers to competency and scenario questions

When discussing your competencies, it's important that you back up your statements. In other words, explain *how* you developed the skills and attributes that you claim to possess. It's also key that you give proper context about each experience, and this is something that people often forget. Don't assume that the reader or interviewer will have any background knowledge about you, the organisations you have contributed to, and the nature of the roles you highlight. So with this in mind, I'll talk through a structure that I find to be particular effective when discussing competencies.

If you're working on a "why you" type question, or the "why you" section of a cover letter, you could start with an introductory sentence, for example "I believe I have developed a foundation of the key skills required of commercial lawyers...". You could then back this statement up by talking through a number of your experiences, including what you did and the skills you developed from each. And this applies equally when discussing a specific competency that you're asked about.

1. As mentioned, start by giving context about the organisation and your position.

Was the organisation international, regional, high street, or university-based? If it's a professional services firm, is it full-service or boutique? Does it have a particular specialism? Is it highly regarded (this can be a particularly important point to make if you've worked abroad, as graduate recruiters might not have heard of it)?

Were you employed, freelancing or volunteering? Part-time or full-time? Were you selected through a competitive process? Elected? Invited to participate? For example, you might say *"Whilst employed full-time as a paralegal at Organisation Z, a regional full-service law firm, I..."* or *"As the elected president of X Society, which aims to enhance access to the legal profession, I..."*.

> **Practical tip:** note that using words such as "elected", "selected" and "invited" can help to show that somebody else identified something special about you, and this led to them picking you over other people. This can help to give you credibility and set you apart from others.

2. Next, explain what your role or contribution involved.

Use "I" rather than "we" where possible, as they want to know about you specifically. For example: *"I... was responsible for drafting transaction documents such as powers of attorney and board minutes, as well as project managing due diligence processes, signings and completions"*. Or *"I...was responsible for recruiting and managing a committee of 10, growing the society's member base, sourcing speakers for events, and creating resources to facilitate members' professional development"*.

3. Finally, highlight the skills that your contributions enabled you to develop or demonstrate

For example: *"This experience... honed my attention to detail, developed my project management skills, refined my communication skills, demonstrated my ability to work effectively in a team whilst under pressure, or required an ability to interact professionally with clients"*. At this stage, in the context of a "why you" type question, you could then elaborate further on your first experience, by drawing out other aspects of the role (and the corresponding skills you developed or demonstrated), or you could move onto the next experience.

Give context about the organisation and your position	Explain what *your* role or contribution involved	Highlight the skills you developed/ demonstrated	Elaborate on this experience, or move onto another experience

When deciding which skills to draw out for "why you" type questions, perhaps check the firm's website to see which key skills they highlight, then try to cover these off. If instead you're asked about one specific competency, then focus on skills relating to that competency. For example. if asked specifically about team working skills, perhaps focus on directly related skills such as your ability to effectively: communicate, delegate, adapt, interact positively with team members, motivate others, and build relationships, as opposed to less relevant attributes such as attention to detail and legal acumen.

Practical tip: when progressing through this answer structure, it's important to make sure that the aspects of your role that you choose to highlight *actually* evidence the skills you decide to mention. If these two elements of your answer don't align (i.e. the explanation of your role + the skills you link to this role), then the recruiter might not be convinced that you've actually developed the skills you've highlighted. Essentially, you can't assume that a graduate recruiter will naturally draw the conclusion that a certain experience will automatically have resulted in you developing a particular skill.

For example, if you mention that you've drafted legal documents, then it's pretty clear that this would have required some level of legal acumen and attention to detail. However, if you link this aspect of your role to a skill such as teamworking, the link is not quite so obvious, meaning your answer might therefore fail to convince a recruiter that you can work effectively in a team. If, conversely, you're asked to demonstrate your ability to work in a team, then consider which aspects of the role you choose to discuss helped to facilitate effective teamwork, and focus on these (for a detailed example of how to do this, check out the below section on teamworking skills).

The STAR structure

When answering "Tell me about a time..." questions, for instance "Tell me about a time when you have...successfully tackled a challenge, had to manage competing responsibilities, worked successfully in a team, successfully undertaken a leadership role..." and so on, the STAR approach to answering questions could be worth bearing in mind. STAR stands for Situation – Task – Action – Result, and I'll now cover each element in turn.

1. Situation

When discussing the situation, you should start by setting the scene. In other words, give *context*. For example: "*Whilst at university, I was President of the Finance Society, which aimed to enhance members' commercial awareness and employability through delivering workshops and arranging networking opportunities*". If you are answering a question on teamwork, perhaps explain what led to you joining the team. For a question on leadership, explain how you ended up in a leadership position (e.g. were you elected?).

2. Task

Next, you could explain your (or your team's) designated task or role, for instance: "My team was tasked with arranging a ball for 400 people". When elaborating on this, consider explaining what you set out to achieve, whether you were set a tight deadline, whether you faced any challenges (if so, explain *why* the circumstances posed a challenge), and so on.

3. Action

This is the most substantial part of the answer and requires you to explain what *you* actually did to complete the task, how you went about doing it, why you did it, how you solved any issues, and the skills you used or developed whilst taking such action. You need to distinguish between *your* contributions and those of others; the employer will likely have little interest in what others did, so try to avoid repeatedly using "we".

4. Result

Conclude by explaining the impact your actions had and what you actually managed to achieve. Make sure you're prepared to discuss what you learned and what you could have done differently, and give statistics where possible. For example "*my contributions led to x% member growth, the sale of x number of tickets, me winning x competition*", and so on.

As you've probably noticed, the STAR approach is fairly similar to the more general approach we discussed for answering competency questions. However, the STAR structure is a little more rigid, plus it requires you to highlight a particular result or outcome, meaning it isn't always applicable. This is especially the case when you're asked a question that isn't centred on a specific task or doesn't require you to highlight a particular result or outcome, plus it's not usually relevant to motivation questions either. I realise that some firms and career advisers at times imply that you should *always* try to use the STAR structure, but I think the point they're more trying to get across is that you always need to give context.

Tell me about a time...you managed competing responsibilities

To demonstrate how to utilise the STAR structure, let's look at the question "Tell me about a time when you had to manage competing responsibilities". You would first want to explain the **situation** – i.e. the context of your role – for example "I was volunteering part-time at my university's pro bono commercial law clinic". You would then want to highlight the **task** you were set, or in this case, the various tasks that led to you having to manage competing responsibilities. For example, perhaps you were working on multiple small transactions or categories of small claims for a variety of clients, each with different deadlines.

Next, you would want to explain the **actions** you took, and in the context of this question, those actions should demonstrate that you know how to effectively balance competing responsibilities. To give some examples, you could start by saying that you were aware of the importance of communication when balancing work for different supervisors. You could explain that when someone tried to delegate work to you, you first asked for some time to ensure that you would actually be able to meet their deadline in light of your other work commitments (which shows that you took a more considered approach). You might then have let the person know what else you have on and the corresponding deadlines you had been set by other supervisors. Then perhaps asked them (and your other supervisors) whether there was any flexibility with their deadlines (which in practice there often is).

By involving your supervisors in the decision-making, you're less likely to let anyone down (including clients), so indicating that this is the approach you would take can reflect positively on you. After all, as a junior, you may be unaware of what has been promised to clients and how your work fits into the bigger picture, so are not usually best placed to make these kinds of decisions unilaterally. Some people might instead be tempted to simply state that they would work through the night to ensure they got through everything. However, although this approach might reflect positively on your work ethic, working whilst tired can affect the quality of your work and should be avoided if it's not absolutely necessary. Then finally, you would want to explain the **result**, for example "As a result, we successfully resolved multiple client matters within the deadlines, and received three glowing testimonials".

How to answer common competency and strengths-based questions

Once you have reflected on your key experiences and identified the competencies and strengths that you have derived from each, you'll then need to consider how this all might be assessed on an application form or during an interview. When doing so, it can be helpful to bear in mind why these competencies and strengths are relevant, how you can demonstrate them, and what to cover when doing so. Note that the level of detail included below might only be relevant if you're asked distinct, long-form questions about a particular competency or strength. It can be okay to take a higher level approach if, for example, highlighting a broad range of skills in a cover letter or as part of your answer to a more general question such as "why should we hire you?".

Competency questions

Competency questions tend to focus upon your ability to showcase the skills that are necessary to succeed in your chosen career. They will typically require you to explain how you *developed* key skills through your previous experiences, or how your experiences required you to *apply* the necessary skills. Below is a guide to the key competencies and strengths that firms tend to look for in candidates, each with an explanation of why they may be necessary to help you effectively fulfil the role to which you are applying.

Teamwork and interpersonal skills

Q. Discuss a time when you have worked in a team.

Q. How would you deal with a team member that is not pulling their weight?

Q. Have you ever had to boost the morale of a team member? If so, what strategies did you use?

Q. When have you had to deal with a difficult or stressful situation whilst working in a team?

Q. How do you ensure that your voice is heard in a group situation?

Many City careers involve employees having to regularly work in teams. This may be internally within their particular departments; with other internal departments that are working on the same projects; with employees working in other offices within the global network of offices (if the firm is international); and/or with other types of firms. For instance, many transactions involve input from investment banks, law firms, accountancy firms, consultancy firms, regulators and institutional investors, and these different industry players must coordinate effectively in order to successfully execute those transactions.

Firms will therefore need to ensure that you'll be able to interact effectively with colleagues, contribute positively to the firm's culture, and act professionally and courteously when representing the firm to clients and in your dealings with third party organisations. Which is why many firms test your ability to work in teams during assessment centres and internships. So how can you demonstrate these skills? For starters, recounting the ways in which you've succeeded in team-based situations – even if your examples aren't drawn from a professional context – can help to shed light on your ability to work effectively with others.

> **Hannah Salton explains how you can demonstrate teamworking skills:** think about various times when you have worked as part of a team. University group projects provide an obvious example, but you may also have worked in a team when volunteering, carrying out work experience, attending internships or working with university societies. Reflect on examples involving challenging dynamics or interesting contexts, for example times where conflicts or unexpected challenges have arisen, or where there have been stark differences in the preferred working styles of different team members. Reflect on the role you played in these examples, including how you interacted with others.

Jake Schogger's tips: when discussing teamwork, consider mentioning some of the techniques that you used to ensure success (I like to refer to these as the "mechanics" of teamwork). To give a few examples:

- Communication is key to effective teamwork, so perhaps discuss any examples where you established clear and regular channels of communication, kept track of progress, and encouraged team members to share ideas, feedback and opinions. To bring the examples to life, you could go into specifics – for instance by mentioning that you set up a Slack channel, Facebook or WhatsApp group, recurring Zoom meetings, and so on – to facilitate regular communication. You could also mention examples of where you had to use different forms of communication with different stakeholders. For example, let's say you were leading a team responsible for organising an event, and that event also involved coordinating volunteers on the day. In this scenario, perhaps you set up digital communication channels for team members, to facilitate quick and regular communication between those responsible for organising the event and dealing with any issues that arose (in the knowledge that responsiveness would be key). However, for volunteers, perhaps you instead decided to create and circulate clear and comprehensive written instructions at the outset to ensure that those volunteers understood what was expected of them (and to avoid your team having to answer the same questions multiple times).

- Delegation is another key aspect of teamworking. Effective delegation can help a team to work more efficiently, by ensuing work is distributed in a way that ensures nobody is overburdened (and therefore that everyone is able to complete their work on time). It can also ensure that tasks are completed by those with the skills and experience needed to do a good job. To demonstrate that you've acquired and practised this skill, perhaps highlight instances where you've encouraged team members to discuss their skills and experiences, then allocated tasks that play to each person's strengths (and align with their capacity). In addition, mentioning that you actively put yourself forward for particular tasks (including tasks that you knew wouldn't be popular with other team members) can help to further demonstrate that you're a real team player.

- Adaptability is also important, especially when working with people who have different working styles, preferences and attitudes. Demonstrating that you've successfully navigated such differences in the past can evidence your ability to work well with others.

- Effective teamwork can also depend on the motivation and confidence of each team member, including you! Think about whether you've actively motivated others in a group scenario, for example by staying upbeat to maintain a positive atmosphere, encouraging others to contribute and take ownership over their work, trying hard to draw out a diverse range of ideas, and leading by example through pulling your weight and remaining reliable and responsive.

- Relationship building can be another key aspect of teamworking. If you've previously worked with people who you hadn't known at the time, what did you do to break the ice and build that initial rapport? Did you arrange coffees or a team social? If you collaborated with people from different academic or professional disciplines (e.g. for a group project involving lawyers and engineers), did you suggest anything creative to ensure the team works cohesively? For example, did you suggest temporary role swaps so that team members could understand the role of the other disciplines and if so, did this help to ensure you were all truly aligned and able to contribute ideas across disciplines?

Leadership ability

Q. Tell me about a time when you've had to lead a team.

Q. What challenges have you faced when carrying out a leadership role, and how did you deal with them?

As you progress through your career, you are likely to move into more of a managerial role. This can involve responsibility for delegating work, leading and motivating large teams, training juniors, recruiting the right people, ensuring projects are completed on time and to the standards expected, and so on. Although you might not be afforded this level of responsibility until further down the line, firms still need to know that once your career progresses, you'll be able to step up and effectively lead others. And highlighting at least some foundational leadership experience can go some way to convincing firms that you'll rise to the challenge. Note that leadership and teamwork are intertwined, as both competencies require an ability to work effectively with others.

Hannah Salton explains how you can demonstrate leadership skills: think of the qualities you associate with a great leader and reflect on when you have displayed such qualities across a variety of contexts and environments. For example, you may think that strong leaders motivate and inspire others, and you might have demonstrated such qualities when experiencing low member engagement as president of a university society, or whilst captaining a losing sports team. You may think that active listening and clear communication are essential to leadership, and may have demonstrated these skills when mentoring others.

Jake Schogger's tips: when discussing leadership experience, try to draw out some of the key characteristics of effective leadership, if only to demonstrate your awareness of these. For example, you might discuss instances in which you have motivated others, led by example, delegated effectively, built and managed a cohesive team, and so on. If you haven't been elected or hired into a leadership role, perhaps you could highlight an experience where you had to *assume* a leadership role. For example, have you previously worked within a team that wasn't particularly focused or was running out of steam, and did you consequently decide to take the reins and get everyone back on track? If you mention experience motivating others, perhaps explain *how* you did this. Did you lead by example? Help them to see the bigger picture? Encourage them to take ownership over their roles (e.g. by giving them more autonomy)? Did you give them more responsibility to reward their effort and performance? And did you ensure they had sufficient access to any guidance and resources needed to support their role?

Dealing with conflict

Q. Tell me about a time where you dealt effectively with a conflict.

Q. How do you handle difficult people?

Q. Have you had to work with someone whose working style clashed with your own? If so, how did you deal with this?

A whole host of conflicts can arise throughout your career, for example: conflicts with clients, perhaps where they take issue with the quality of work delivered or the bill; conflicts with colleagues, who may be tired and stressed, or have different opinions about how to move forward; and conflicts with people from other firms, for example during negotiations. And such conflicts can escalate unnecessarily if not dealt with appropriately. For this reason, firms may test your ability to resolve conflicts. Note that questions relating to teamwork might also cover your ability to deal with conflicts in group scenarios.

How can you demonstrate your ability to deal with conflict?

Think about times where you've disagreed with others, had to de-escalate a situation, tried to reach a compromise with others (or helped others to reach a compromise), or tried to resolve a dispute. Perhaps, for example, you were part of a university executive committee that was divided over a particular issue, or you worked on a group project and there was a disagreement between group members. Note that it probably wouldn't come across particularly well if you use an example where the other person was totally and objectively in the wrong, as stating this might make you seem stubborn and inflexible. Conflict resolution is all the more impressive where the various parties each had at least a few reasonable requirements or motivations that had to be taken into account when trying to find common ground.

When discussing your ability to deal with conflict, highlight the strategies you used when doing so. For example, did you start by asking open questions so that you could try to understand where each person was coming from? Did you then demonstrate empathy, by explaining that you understand others' opinions, and take the time to calmly explain your own position? Did you then take active steps to work collaboratively with others to resolve the issue or reach a compromise? And were you self-reflecting throughout, to try to determine whether there was anything you had done to unnecessarily cause the conflict (and if so, were you willing to concede or apologise, and did you learn your lesson?).

Negotiation skills

Q. Discuss a time when you have had to negotiate.

Q. When have you had to bring someone else around to your way of thinking?

Somewhat linked to your ability to deal with conflict is your ability to negotiate (both can involve working with others to achieve a compromise), and this ability can be essential throughout your career. It's important if you're a lawyer negotiating contractual clauses or settlement agreements, a consultant negotiating deadlines, a director in an investment bank negotiating fees with a client, a start-up negotiating costs with suppliers, prospective employees negotiating the terms of their employment, and so on.

How can you demonstrate negotiation skills?

"Negotiating" can mean many different things. It might mean trying to secure a price reduction or better terms, but it can also mean bringing someone around to your way of thinking or persuading someone to pursue a particular course of action. Above all, it involves trying to achieve a compromise. With that in mind, reflect upon your prior experiences and try to identify times where you have worked to achieve a compromise or influenced a particular decision. For example, have you negotiated the price or terms of corporate sponsorship for a club or society, or have you negotiated the price of a team's kit, equipment rental or access to facilities?

When discussing your ability to negotiate, perhaps highlight some of the techniques you used to achieve success. For example, you could highlight that you took a cooperative and collaborative approach, with the aim of negotiating "with", not "against" the other side. An approach that focused on interests rather than positions and power tactics, in order to draw out areas of commonality and compatibility. As part of this, perhaps you asked open questions to promote active discussions – and listened attentively so that you could try to understand where the other side was coming from – in order to source the information needed to propose solutions that everyone could get behind. This kind of example could help to show your awareness that in a negotiation, information is king.

Organisation and time-management skills

Q. How do you stay organised?

Q. How do you manage your time and prioritise tasks?

Q. Tell me about a time when you have had to juggle multiple commitments or demands.

City workers are typically expected to be *very* well organised, as they'll often be juggling multiple projects for a number of clients and supervisors, managing various competing deadlines (some of which may be brought forward with little warning), coordinating numerous internal and external teams and advisers, and working on a wide range of unfamiliar documents and processes. Organisation and time-management skills, including the ability to prioritise (and re-prioritise), are therefore fundamental.

How can you demonstrate organisation and time-management skills?

Start by arriving on time for an interview! That aside, think about times where you've had to juggle a variety of competing responsibilities. This could include working part-time whilst studying, balancing various positions of responsibility, or committing to time-intensive extra-curricular activities (e.g. ones that involve regular training sessions or performances). When discussing organisation skills, perhaps highlight the methods you used to stay organised and effectively juggle your responsibilities. For example, did you use calendar appointments and reminders (e.g. for recurring tasks), a notebook for detailed notes, a high level to-do list to help you prioritise, or a particular email filing system to keep on top of everything? Did you regularly reflect on what needs to be done, to check you're on track? I was once asked to explain in detail how I prioritise my time, and ended up showing the interviewer a copy of my calendar and task list to demonstrate my approach to organisation. You could also discuss a time where you've had to adjust your schedule to manage unexpected responsibility, for example if a team member dropped out of their role on short notice and you had to find a way to pick up the slack. On a similar note, if you're ever asked to discuss how you manage competing responsibilities, keep in mind the considerations outlined in my above example of how to use the STAR structure.

Analytical skills and attention to detail

Q. When have you had to pay close attention to detail?

Q. When have you demonstrated analytical skills when tackling a problem?

The work carried out by City firms can require individuals to review, process and advise on vast amounts of complex information. Strong analytical skills and attention to detail are therefore of vital importance – whether you are drafting contracts, inputting figures into financial models, drafting emails to clients or proofreading documents for supervisors – as even the smallest mistakes can have far reaching consequences. For example, mistakes could result in financial losses for a client and liability for the firm, whilst having a negative impact on the firm's client relationships and broader reputation. Mistakes can also negatively impact your personal brand by leading to supervisors perceiving you as unprofessional and unreliable.

How can you demonstrate analytical skills and attention to detail?

Avoid making broad, unsupported statements about having great analytical skills and attention to detail, as this won't come across as credible. Instead, think about times where you've had to really concentrate to analyse information effectively and ensure that the work was completed accurately. This could include, for example, times where you had to maintain detailed spreadsheets to keep track of budgets and spending (e.g. as a university society treasurer), review vast amounts of information and distil it into a report or assignment (e.g. for a dissertation or group project), or produce documents where mistakes could have resulted in liability (e.g. legal documents or financial accounts). Then explain the measures you put in place to ensure accuracy. For example, did you set aside sufficient time to enable you to distance yourself from the work before checking it one final time, or did you seek feedback from others so you could benefit from fresh pairs of eyes?

Ability to problem solve and think laterally/innovatively

Q. When have you had to think outside of the box?

Q. Tell me about a time when you have had to come up with an innovative solution to a problem.

Top City firms charge substantial amounts for their services and clients are increasingly instructing them only when they have particularly challenging and unique issues to resolve or strategies to execute. Firms therefore want candidates who are able to think creatively and laterally to ensure client problems are tackled effectively.

Hannah Salton explains how you can demonstrate problem-solving skills: think about times you have experienced challenges, both big and small. This could be, for example, a time where you worked with complicated information that you had to analyse methodically in order to try and resolve certain issues, a challenge you experienced whilst leading a personal initiative such as a volunteering project, or in the context of an academic project.

Jake Schogger's tips: whatever example you use, try to identify one or more specific issues or challenges that you came up against, then explain how you thought creatively to resolve or circumvent those issues or challenges. It could be, for example, that you suggested a new process for your team to follow, carried out research into alternative ways of working, or even came up with a totally "outside the box" suggestion. Either way, be clear as to what the "problem" was, and how you "solved" it.

Adaptability, flexibility and cultural awareness

Q. Have you ever had to demonstrate adaptability to meet expectations?

Q. Have you ever had to adapt your usual approach when interacting with others?

City workers may be expected to work for and interact with a broad range of people, each of whom might come from different backgrounds, communicate, interact and approach work in different ways, and have differing working styles and preferences.

In addition, working hours and deadlines can be unpredictable and circumstances can change at a moment's notice. Adaptability, flexibility and cultural awareness, including an ability to adapt your communication and working styles (as well as your schedule) when necessary, can therefore be essential. Note that there's often overlap between adaptability and communication skills.

> **How can you demonstrate adaptability, flexibility and cultural awareness?**
>
> Think about times where the circumstances have required you to adapt your usual approach to interacting with others or carrying out responsibilities. For example, have you worked in a team where you had to adapt to a range of different personalities or working styles? Or whilst mentoring or tutoring younger students, did you have to adapt your approach to communicating educational concepts to cater to different age groups, abilities, or backgrounds? Have you faced an unexpected challenge or change in circumstance that required you to change course in some way? If so, make sure you are able to explain *how* you adapted your approach, and how doing so contributed to a positive outcome.

Communication skills, presentation skills, networking skills and confidence

> **Q.** Discuss a time when you have delivered a presentation to a large audience.
>
> **Q.** When have you had to utilise effective communication skills?
>
> **Q.** Tell me about a time when you have benefitted from networking with others.

Many City careers involve presenting to and regularly liaising with clients, other firms, and employees within your firm. Confidence and communication skills are therefore important, as is an ability to deliver engaging, professional and concise presentations. Moreover, as you become more senior, you may be expected to bring work into the firm and this is often facilitated through networking, so an ability to make connections and build relationships can also be key.

> **Hannah Salton explains how you can show these skills:** think about times you've had difficult conversations or had to communicate with those that are very different from you. Have you worked with people from a different background to you? Have you delivered any presentations on a specialist subject? Or been responsible for a social media platform? You could also mention public speaking experience (e.g. debating or mooting) or times you have delivered public performances.
>
> **Jake Schogger's tips:** think of instances where you have been tasked with communicating effectively with others, be that in writing or verbally, one-on-one or to a room full of people. This could include, for example, communicating whilst networking, public speaking (e.g. delivering a presentation or participating in a moot or debate), delivering training or providing instructions (e.g. if whilst working in a shop you had to show new recruits how everything works), negotiating (e.g. with suppliers on behalf of a university society), interacting with customers, writing formal documents (e.g. whilst working at a pro bono clinic), and so on. Next, consider the "communication" aspects of your experiences. For example, did you need to adapt your communication style (e.g. based on the seniority or background of the recipients of your communications)? Or did you have to find a way to communicate something complex in an easily digestible manner? If so, did you come up with a creative way of achieving this?

Commitment, motivation, ambition and drive

> **Q.** When have you demonstrated commitment in the face of adversity?
>
> **Q.** When have you excelled under pressure?

City work can be very demanding, and firms will want to know that you will stick around, even when you're facing long hours and tackling less interesting work. They will also want to see evidence that you'll be able to rise to the challenge and excel under such circumstances. Demonstrating that you've been able to commit to tasks in the past can help to prove that you are a worthy candidate, as can evidencing your ongoing commitment to personal and professional development.

> **How can you demonstrate commitment, motivation, ambition and drive?**
>
> Think about times where you've voluntarily committed to something time-intensive. This could include training sessions for a sports team, years of rehearsals for a dance, music or theatre club, mentoring sessions, or a whole host of other extra-curricular activities. Positions of responsibility (e.g. running university societies) can also provide great examples to demonstrate these attributes. After all, choosing to spend your free time doing something interesting or productive requires at least some level of motivation and drive. Doing this regularly also requires commitment, whilst if you're challenging yourself at the same time, there's your ambition. Moreover, if you continued to commit to a responsibility even in the face of or personal pressure (e.g. stress brought on by the pandemic) or adversity (e.g. if you experienced an injury, but worked through your recovery and continued with a sport), this can help to further demonstrate your drive, as well as your resilience.

Ability to work under pressure

> **Q.** When have you had to work under pressure to meet a tight deadline?
>
> **Q.** How do you react under pressure?

When deadlines are tight or things go wrong, City careers can involve working under immense pressure to meet client expectations, so firms will likely want to know that you're able to stay composed and productive when you're up against it.

How can you demonstrate your ability to work under pressure?

Think about times where you've really been up against it. This might have been because of a tight deadline and the sheer magnitude of what you needed to do. Or perhaps you were particularly challenged by the complexity of your role and had to deliver something to an incredibly high standard with no room for error. The experiences you could draw from might include, for example, working on a group project or academic assignment, or preparing for, delivering or participating in a large event, performance, debate, mock trial or pitch. When discussing examples, explain how you managed to succeed despite the pressure you were under. For example, did you make time to exercise or take short breaks to help with your composure? Or do you naturally get an adrenaline kick from working with others towards a common goal with a deadline looming?

Client-facing skills

Q. When have you worked in a service role?

Q. When have you had to interact professionally with others?

Q. Have you ever worked in a client-facing role?

Many City roles are client-facing. Whether you're a lawyer, investment banker, accountant or a consultant, you're providing a service to a paying client on behalf of your employer, and you therefore need to be able to act professionally when doing so.

How can you demonstrate client-facing skills?

As mentioned earlier, the word "client" is synonymous with "customer", so any experience involving you interacting positively with customers can help to demonstrate that you're able to act professionally when representing a business. For example, you could discuss experiences where you've worked in a bar or hotel (your "clients" were the patrons), in a retail store or on supermarket checkouts (your "clients" were the shoppers), as a tutor (your "clients" were the tutees and perhaps their parents), and so on. To give context around your role, perhaps mention if you had to deal with, for example, customer complaints, difficult individuals, a broad range of stakeholders, or rude or drunk people. If you haven't had direct experience interacting with customers, then perhaps draw on an analogous role. For example, if you had a leadership role for a university society or sports team, you could discuss your responsibility for ensuring that the members received adequate support, were effectively engaged, and had a positive experience (as people are expected to do with customers).

When discussing client-facing skills, explain the strategies and mindset you adopted to ensure you interacted positively with clients. For example, did you use your adaptability to ensure you communicated effectively with a broad range of people (young, old, students, professionals, happy, angry etc.)? Were you consciously aware at all times that you were representing the organisation, so acted courteously and professionally at all times in the knowledge that your actions reflected on the brand of that organisation? Did you note down facts about regular clients so that you could strike up polite conversations and meet any particular requirements or expectations they had? Did you remain outwardly composed, enthusiastic and empathetic, even when dealing with complaints or difficult situations? Did you dress professionally, show up punctually, work efficiently, and meet all your deadlines?

Proactivity/initiative

Q. Tell me about a time where you have demonstrated initiative?

Q. Have you ever had to go above and beyond the call of duty to get things done?

City firms want to hire people who are able to use their initiative, be resourceful, and remain proactive. These characteristics are key in high pressure, client-led environments – where people are generally busy and the work is intellectually challenging – as they can suggest an individual will be able to learn quickly, complete more work autonomously, and consequently contribute more effectively (in part, through making their supervisors' lives easier).

How can you demonstrate initiative and proactivity?

Try to think about times where you've gone the extra mile to make something happen or figure something out by yourself. For example, have you ever spent hours in your free time voluntarily learning a new skill, software programme or process – or reading up on industries and clients – in order to get up to speed and enhance your performance at work? Maybe you suggested a new way of working in order to boost your team's productivity, or put yourself forward for certain opportunities (for example, by offering to deliver training to others on some new development). Or do you have examples from other work experiences where you've taken certain actions in anticipation of follow-on tasks (even if just drafting a cover email for your supervisor to use when sending your work to a client)?

Resilience and dealing with rejection

Q. Tell me about a time when you have failed at something and then bounced back.

Q. Discuss a time when you've been rejected, received negative feedback, or something hasn't gone your way. How did this affect you and how did you respond?

Q. When have you succeeded in the face of adversity?

Q. What is your biggest failure?

During a graduate scheme, you are likely to receive constructive criticism/feedback on an almost daily basis, yet people may be too busy to acknowledge when you've excelled or to thank you for your work. Firms need to know that this won't lead to you sulking or giving up; they want to hire people that will respond actively and positively to negative feedback by continually pushing themselves to improve. People with a mindset that enables them to remain positive and enthusiastic, even when things go wrong or they're in a stressful situation. And this all requires resilience.

How can you demonstrate resilience?

When answering a question on resilience or rejection, it's fine to mention negative feedback that you've previously received, as long as you can demonstrate that you responded positively and adapted your approach in light of that feedback. It's also fine to discuss a time you failed or experienced a setback, as long as you can demonstrate that you picked yourself back up again. Perhaps explain the context, then focus on the actions you took to surmount or mitigate the setback or failure. For example, I mentioned failing to get into the university football team (my response was to set up my own 5-a-side team, so that I could still play regularly), being rejected for a position on the Law Society executive committee (after which I set up a commercial law-focused society, so I could still experience running a university society), and struggling with one particular academic module (which led to me actively seeking regular feedback on how to improve). And these answers went down well.

Note that commercial awareness is another competency that firms may test. However, we cover this in more detail in the *Commercial Awareness* chapter, including what it means and how you can demonstrate it, so haven't covered it here.

Common ethical questions

Q. When have you acted ethically?

Q. When have you done something ethically questionable?

Q. Is it ever justifiable to lie?

Q. Would you report a colleague if you realised that they had made a mistake?

Q. Would you support a client's lie or mistake if to do otherwise would mean the firm loses the client?

Q. Should your client pay a bribe if necessary to get the job done?

Q. Would you ever pay a ransom?

Firms may ask ethical questions to gain a greater insight into your character. Alternatively, they may simply want to test how you react under pressure and deal with difficult questions. There are not necessarily "correct" answers to all ethical questions, but remember, professional ethics are *absolute*. Firms want to ensure their employees always act with integrity; there is no leeway!

How can you demonstrate ethics?

Of course, answers to ethical questions will very much depend on the nature of the question. If you're asked whether you've acted ethically in the past, you might be able to talk about times you've acted honestly (e.g. handed in a phone or money you've found on the floor, or come clean about a mistake you've made). You could also highlight charitable initiatives that you support, or provide examples of where you have made a positive contribution for free (for example, whilst volunteering, mentoring, or carrying out pro bono work).

Questions regarding how you would react if you found out a team member had made a mistake can be particularly tricky. In general, you might want to first consider the nature of the mistake, then approach the person about it and (if possible) offer to help them rectify it. If the mistake cannot be rectified by the individual, then perhaps you would recommend that they come clean. And if they don't, maybe you should then report it. Ultimately, you want to ensure that the firm doesn't face avoidable liability. If you face a scenario that's a little vague, consider asking your interviewer questions to help shape your answer, for example "has the mistake been caught early enough to be rectified by the individual?", or "it is firm policy that a mistake of that nature should be reported to a supervisor?".

Common strengths and weakness-based questions

What are strengths-based questions?

A strength is essentially a competency that you have developed to a high standard, *and actually enjoy utilising*. In contrast, if you're good at something but don't enjoy doing it, this likely wouldn't constitute a strength. In light of this, strengths-based questions tend to be used to assess not just your capability to fulfil a role, but your overall *suitability* to the role. These questions usually centre upon how you behave or react in certain situations, which can provide firms with an insight into your character, your proficiencies and what you enjoy doing. And this in turn can enable firms to gauge whether your strengths align with the role for which you are applying. In other words, firms want to make sure you're not only able to complete particular tasks well, but also that such tasks make you tick.

Why do firms care? Well, evidence indicates that people who use their strengths at work are generally happier, more confident, more engaged, more resilient (and therefore less stressed), more effective at developing themselves, more likely to perform well and achieve their goals, and more likely to have high levels of energy and self-esteem. So if your strengths align with the types of tasks you will likely be completing on a day-to-day basis, this could indicate that you'll stay energised and focused when completing those tasks, you'll enjoy the work to a greater extent, you'll learn faster and perform better, and you'll remain enthusiastic and motivated (which is important if you need to work long hours!). Conversely, if you're clearly able to complete particular tasks but those tasks don't align with your strengths, this could suggest that regularly engaging in such work could tire you out and negatively affect your motivation and performance.

There is no point in lying when answering these questions, as you can never be certain of the answer firms are expecting. Moreover, if your honest answers truly indicate that you would be unsuited to (and potentially miserable in) such a role, then it is probably best for both you and the prospective employer if your application does not progress. With all this in mind, below are some examples of the types of questions you may be asked, along with an explanation of why those questions can be important.

Q. What are your strengths?

As mentioned above, getting to know your strengths can help a firm to gauge not only your capability to fulfil the role, but your overall suitability to the role. If the nature of the work you'll be carrying out aligns with your strengths, this suggests you're more likely to remain engaged, motivated and enthusiastic.

Q. What motivates you?

The things that motivate you can indicate to a firm whether you are likely to enjoy (and consequently be energised by) the type of work you would carry out if you were offered a graduate role. Good answers I have previously come across included statements such as: "I am motivated by my desire to: secure achievements that truly challenge me on both a personal and intellectual level; constantly learn and develop in order to reach my full potential; stand out from a crowd; be the best I can possibly be" and so on, followed by examples of where the candidate had taken positive action to help achieve these aims.

Q. What is your biggest weakness?

Firms ask about your weaknesses not just to identify whether they might render you unsuitable for the role, but also to ascertain whether you are self-aware. Of course, nobody likes talking about their weaknesses. However, everyone has weaknesses, so you should never try to claim that you are the exception. If the question does come up, don't try to frame a strength as a weakness. "My biggest weakness is that I'm a perfectionist" won't get you anywhere, as this can show a real lack of self-awareness. Recruiters want to hear an authentic answer, based on genuine self-reflection; they're not simply giving you an opportunity to show off about your perceived perfections.

Think about your weaknesses and how you have addressed them or found a way to work around them. Obviously try to avoid discussing a weakness that goes totally against the core competencies required to succeed in the role. If an aspiring lawyer mentions their "complete and utter lack of attention to detail" or a budding accountant admits that they are "terrible with numbers", this probably wouldn't go down too well. Instead, try to identify a weakness that can be easily improved upon and won't reflect too negatively on your ability to succeed from day one.

If you mention a weakness that is rectifiable and then explain how you're working on it on an ongoing basis, this can actually reflect very positively on your character. And highlighting examples where you have deliberately placed yourself outside of your comfort zone to work on a weakness can be particularly effective. For example, if you admit that you lack confidence when public speaking, but highlight that you have joined the debating or mooting club to gain additional public speaking experience and build that confidence, the firm will likely be impressed with your self-awareness and the actions you've taken to improve. Similarly, confidence when networking might be a weakness that doesn't strike at the core of the role, and something you tried to improve by attending numerous networking events (such as career fairs or employer events).

During my training contract, delegation was a particular weakness of mine. I didn't feel comfortable delegating boring/administrative work to paralegals, many of whom were more experienced than I was, and didn't know how to ensure I was delegating clearly and effectively. I dealt with this in two ways. Firstly, by speaking to seniors about how they improved their ability to delegate effectively. Secondly, by seeking feedback from the paralegals to whom I had delegated. I asked for their thoughts on being allocated work and what they saw as "poor" delegation and "great" delegation from others. The paralegals pointed out that if nobody allocated work to them, their job wouldn't exist, and that they chose to be in that role so had no issue with being delegated the types of administrative tasks that paralegals tend to complete. They also gave examples of good and bad delegation, which I then kept in mind when subsequently preparing to delegate. This all really helped me to get over my discomfort and improve my technique, which actually improved my working relationships with paralegals.

Another weakness of mine was – and still is, to some extent – speaking too quickly when excited or nervous, and this has been the case since I was a child (I have often received feedback to this effect, first from grandparents, then from City trainers and attendees at my events!). So I took positive action to improve my presentation skills. Essentially, I repeatedly recorded myself speaking, listened back, adjusted my pace, then tried again, until I became more familiar with how the "right" pace feels.

Questions may alternatively focus on how successful you are at carrying out certain tasks, how often you complete those tasks, and how you *feel* when doing so. And your answers to these questions may provide the firm with an insight into how you are likely to respond and perform in the role for which you are applying. Have a think about which of your strengths align best with the firm and the role for which you are applying, and consider how to evidence these strengths during an interview.

In particular, try linking your strengths to your previous experiences, focusing on your behaviours and actions that evidenced those strengths. Also be prepared to discuss how you feel when demonstrating these strengths, how often you utilise them, and how successful you are when doing so. With this in mind, below are examples of the strengths and character insights firms may assess, alongside the types of behaviours and actions they may ask you about when doing so. Detailed discussion of each is outside the scope of this handbook, but it's worth considering your answers in advance of any interviews that might include a strengths-related discussion. To further aid your preparation, you can also access a free strengths assessment at www.jobmi.com.

Drive and ambition

Q. Do you push yourself to get things done and succeed, regardless of setbacks?

Q. Have you worked long hours to deliver work to a high quality and standard?

Q. Do you prefer doing things that give you a sense of purpose?

Personal development

Q. Do you test yourself in new, unfamiliar or difficult situations?

Q. Do you actively try to seek out new knowledge and information?

Q. Do you tend to learn from mistakes?

Q. In difficult situations, do you take responsibility and act quickly and decisively?

Q. Do you remain balanced and self-assured in stressful situations?

Your attitude

Q. Do you maintain a positive outlook even in difficult circumstances or make jokes to lighten the mood?

Q. Do you stand up for your values and what you believe in?

Your approach to work

Q. Do you tend to plan ahead and organise well in advance?

Q. Do you focus on the bigger picture or the granular details?

Interactions with others

Q. Are you more likely to learn from, motivate or compete against others?

Q. Are you able to build a rapport with people quickly and easily?

Q. Do you tend to listen intently to, help and support others in difficult circumstances?

Q. Do you appreciate and value the role of others in your successes and give credit to others when it's due?

Type of work you find engaging

Q. Do you enjoy inventing something new or developing a different way of doing things?

Q. Do you enjoy spotting and rectifying errors, or pre-empting issues that may arise and mitigating them in advance?

Further insights into your character and thought process

Some interview questions may be used as icebreakers or to provide an insight into your thought processes. Below are some examples of questions that you may be asked.

Q. Tell me about...

You may be asked to talk about one of the experiences mentioned on your CV or in your application. This can involve a more conversational approach, so don't necessarily try to highlight as many skills as possible. Just talking enthusiastically and in detail about your experiences will enable the interviewer to ascertain how those experiences supported your personal development.

Q. What do you typically do when you have time off?

An insight into how you spend your free time can help a firm to ascertain whether you're the kind of person who is committed to personal development. For example, if you actively pursue your passions and interests, this might demonstrate your initiative, drive, desire to experience different cultures, and willingness to push yourself by leaving your comfort zone from time to time.

Q. If you had the time and opportunity to learn a new skill, what would it be and why?

This question might be asked to test whether you always have a goal in mind. If you mention a particular skill, you might then be asked to explain why you haven't yet had the chance to pursue it, so give this some thought in advance.

Q. What made you want to study in the UK (if you are an international student)?

This type of question can give the interviewer an insight into your thought process when making serious decisions. If you chose to study abroad, perhaps explain which other countries you had considered and why you eventually made the choice you made. Think about these factors in advance, just to make sure that you can give a detailed answer. Also be prepared to discuss whether you intend to stay in the UK for the long-term and if so, why.

Q. How did you choose your degree?

Again, this question will give the interviewer an insight into how you make decisions. If you chose your degree because of factors that also apply to the career you're pursuing, your answer might also help to reinforce your career motivation. Perhaps explain which sources you used when researching into different universities, and your key reasons for settling on your chosen university.

Q. What influenced your decision to do a Master's degree?

If you have studied (or are studying) a Master's degree, this question may well come up. Interviewers might simply be interested in your reasons for investing the time and money in further study, or may instead be testing your thought process. Be prepared to explain why you thought a Master's degree would benefit you in the longer-term, and to discuss what you enjoyed about it.

Prizes, awards and achievements

Many application forms include a box in which candidates can highlight any additional information or provide a summary of the prizes, awards and achievements they have accumulated. Below are examples of what you could perhaps include.

- Did you receive the top grades at your school or place in the top percentile in Europe/worldwide for a particular subject? Were you asked to be Head Boy/Girl or a Prefect at school? Have you received any bursaries or scholarships?

- Have you reached a sporting, dance, drama or musical instrument milestone (e.g. by passing a particular grade)? Have you won any competitions (be it horse riding or mooting, go kart racing or a virtual stock market challenge)? Have you successfully completed a marathon or climbed a mountain?

- Are you experienced using particular software or technology (e.g. a coding language, Microsoft Office, WestLaw, or Bloomberg terminals)?

Consider whether certain achievements may have occurred too long ago to reflect on your current character and abilities, and perhaps only include older prizes and awards if they are particularly pertinent.

A career advisor's perspective

Claire Leslie, our friendly careers guru and acclaimed career advisor, has helped thousands of students prepare for competency and strengths-based interviews. Here is some advice from Claire on how to tackle some of the trickier questions that come up.

How would your friends describe you?

You might be tempted to relax when facing this question. Perhaps the question conjures up the pleasing image of fun evenings with friends? Don't lose your focus. This isn't the time for the phrase "party animal" to pop out. Thinking about the question in advance of an interview will ensure you are more able to give an impressive reply.

Why is the interviewer asking you the question?

The recruiter is trying to find out as much as possible about you. It's as important to know if you will fit into the existing teams, as it is to know if you can do the job. It's no good recruiting the excellent operator, who upsets everyone else in the workplace and causes all sorts of disruption. It's relevant to know what your friends think about you and indeed to know if you have friends! The way in which you answer this question will give an insight into your self-awareness. How does what you say relate to the impression that the interviewer has formed about you in the interview? If you have come across as quiet and reserved and your answer is "fun and zany" then there is a mismatch. Why might that be? You may just have made the recruiter anxious.

What shouldn't you say?

This isn't the time to come out with a list of attributes you hope the interviewer wants to hear. You might be tempted to go with: "Oh, they think I am very bright and they know that I work really hard and that I am a complete perfectionist". It's not the best answer. This just doesn't sound as if it is the way friends talk about one another. You risk the interviewer deciding that you are being less than completely honest, which could be fatal. Think about what picture your answer is going to give the interviewer. "Fun" gives the impression that you can make others laugh and make a social event go with a swing. The kind of person you might want in a workplace. "Party animal" might be another way of describing the same individual, but the picture it creates is different. I see the late night party, and then worry about the bleary eyed employee the following day.

What sort of words do friends use about one another?

Here are some of the words I would use about my friends: loyal, kind, always there for me, unselfish, funny, honest, practical (or sometimes impractical). The words I use refer to our emotional connection. Of course, many of my friends are also very clever, hard-working and good looking, but these are not the attributes which principally drive and maintain our friendship. You may be thinking: surely the interviewer doesn't want to hear words like this? Well why not? Someone who can be described with some of the words I have used above is probably going to be a good team player, able to fit into the workplace. These are appropriate words which identify key reasons why people choose to be friends, so your answer is more likely to sound genuine and honest. Why not do your research? Ask your friends how they would describe you. See if they are all saying the same thing (sometimes we can behave differently with different people). If the answers are different, think about the real you. Come up with three words so that you are ready for this question. How to deliver the answer? Smile, you're talking about your friends – it makes me happy when I think about mine!

What was your greatest disappointment?

This type of question can give the interviewer an idea of how you handle adversity; the trouble is that you might not have had any significant adversity to deal with, or at least none that you want to share in an interview! So how are you going to answer?

What not to do

You don't want to sound arrogant. Don't go for the wide-eyed look, accompanying an incredulous denial that you have ever been disappointed. This is unlikely to endear you to an interviewer, who probably has encountered one or two setbacks in his or her life. This is also not the time to bring up a genuine disaster. I certainly wouldn't recommend talking about one of life's great griefs like the loss of someone you loved. The emotions involved go far beyond any disappointment and you risk putting the interviewer in an embarrassing position, or worse, upsetting yourself and losing focus.

On the other hand, you should avoid the utterly trivial. "I was disappointed when I burnt my dinner because I was looking forward to eating it" risks a laugh which could just be at you rather than with you! Use this approach only if you can't think of anything else and even then, only to buy yourself a bit more time. Start the laugh yourself. That way you can be sure that you're all laughing together, and you might come across as the sort of person the interviewer would like to have in the office.

Dodging the question altogether is not really an option. The interviewer wants to know that you always learn from disappointment and change your behaviour accordingly. You might accumulate a negative comment on the interviewer's mark sheet if you fail to answer the question properly – definitely worth avoiding! Moreover, some interviewers simply will not let you move onto the next question until you have given an answer.

How can you find the happy compromise?

Start by thinking of an example which will allow you to showcase your resilience and your ability to overcome a problem. The exam which didn't go according to plan might work. You have probably already had to disclose your marks on an application form, so you won't be telling your prospective interviewer anything new. Did your disappointment make you reassess your work ethic, or take advice on how to improve?

Another option might be the disappointing decision you took for the greater good, but you'll have to be careful. It could be useful, for example, to talk about how you gave up an extracurricular activity to focus on your work and about the disappointment this caused you. You won't however want to imply that you do nothing but work! You could also talk about the time you bowed to a majority decision which was at odds with what you wanted, although you need to take care here too. If you ended up in this position, your powers of persuasion obviously didn't work (which might be an issue if you need to be particularly persuasive as part of the role for which you are applying).

It's also quite difficult to talk about what you learnt without potentially sounding petulant. How is the following comment going to go down: *"I did what everyone else wanted against my better judgement and it turned out badly. It proved that I was right all along"*? If you are going to use this example, you'd be better saying: *"I went along with the majority and although I was initially disappointed, it turned out fine. I learnt that it is sometimes important to be prepared to concede a point and that there can be advantages to doing this. It can give you a wholly new perspective on something"*. Whatever you decide on this question, it definitely falls into the category of one you'll want to ponder in advance of the interview.

What is your greatest achievement?

The employer isn't looking for the marathon running, country representing, top-flight musician who has received an Oscar for acting and single-handedly solved the Greek debt crisis! Instead, it is looking for the person who can demonstrate that they have done something other than just study. The answer can be equally impressive if you have spent a gap year persuading reluctant parents in Africa to allow their children to be inoculated against polio.

Start very simply: *"I think my greatest achievement is.../I am most proud of..."* and then set out what you did. Use the STAR framework (explained earlier in this handbook). Describe the circumstances fairly briefly and then focus most of your answer on the action you took, but avoid hyperbole. Finish by highlighting the result and reflecting on the skills you gained. If you attained your achievement whilst working alongside study, then you'll have demonstrated a great work ethic, resilience and time management skills. If you have contributed to society, then you'll want to point out how your efforts have impacted others. If, however, you want to work in a profit-making City organisation, you might want to focus more on the relevant transferable skills you developed. Communication? Teamwork? Persuasion and negotiation?

It's probably not a good idea to tell an investment bank that following your amazing experience working with the dispossessed, you have decided to work for the bank because you like its corporate social responsibility policy. Remember that the bank is "about" making money. Their staff need to buy into that idea. If they think that you just want to "help", they're probably going to wonder if you will be right for them.

> **Jake Schogger's tips:** make sure you give context when answering this question (don't assume that the achievement is self-explanatory). Highlight not only the overall achievement, but *why* it was an achievement. What were the challenges that you overcame? How did you overcome them? Did this require prolonged dedication and resilience? And then don't forget to include the outcome at the end, for example the amount of money you raised, the attendance you achieved, the feedback you received, or the qualification you were awarded.

Tell me about your cultural awareness

In this age of globalisation, cultural awareness is an overarching skill and a necessity. Demonstrating your flexibility, open-mindedness and cultural awareness will always be important. During your time at university you are exposed to new experiences, including a range of different cultures and languages. These enriching learning experiences can be used in your working life. They develop you as a person and make you more employable; in the UK and across the wider world. Have you ever stopped to think about how culturally aware you are? Probably not. Few of us take the time to reflect on our skill sets or consider the gaps in them.

Why is the interviewer asking you the question?

Global companies will want to see that you are open to new ideas and cultures. Can you communicate with people from different nations and avoid ambiguity? Can you build relationships that take account of different cultural expectations and needs? Do you always try to understand and value different perspectives whilst seeking common ground? Will you be able to research new markets and cultures and have the sensitivity to check in with contacts when necessary to get clarification and iron out problems?

How can you demonstrate your cultural awareness?

Languages can be a great asset, but they are only one piece of a complex jigsaw. Networking at university with students from different nationalities can help to give you a better understanding of what is important in their countries. Researching specific markets and countries will give you a chance to identify trends in the global market, whilst appreciating what each nation has to offer. You can also begin to understand the cultural values which sometimes lead to confusion. Checking for clarification is vital, and this is the hidden communication skill that is essential in a global marketplace.

You've probably mixed with people from different cultures, faiths and even picked up the odd words of another language. Perhaps you are the person who has had the confidence to come to another country to learn another language, travel, study abroad or to build new networks. Start thinking about some examples. Reflect on how you have made the best of the multi-cultural environment at university. Don't think that you won't need to worry about this if you're not aspiring to work for an international company. All recruiters want a broad range of skills to equip them to succeed in the global village.

Cultural awareness is about being open to embracing the diversity of life. It is about a willingness to learn, seek new experiences, and ultimately make new friends. It is being open to what life and your career brings you. As you learn to understand more about the world, you'll find there is less certainty. Your cultural awareness will equip you to deal with the situations you and your employer face. So what do you think you've learnt and how will you articulate it? What about discussing flexibility, resilience, interpersonal skills, and accepting ambiguity (understanding there is no one right way).

For advice on scenario-based questions, check out the *Situational judgment tests* section of the *Psychometric Tests* chapter.

Motivation Questions

One of the key attributes sought by City firms is a passion for their businesses. This is because hiring interns, trainees or analysts constitutes a fairly substantial investment for a firm to make. Consider the cost of paying your salary, funding your benefits and covering your expenses; the value of time invested by supervisors training and developing you rather than earning money for the firm; the investment in business support functions (e.g. secretaries, knowledge management, IT, document specialists etc.) to support your role; the cost of arranging socials; and so on.

With this in mind, recruiters want to hire candidates that they believe will accept an offer and remain at the firm for the long-term, if given the opportunity. Long enough for them to start adding real value and generating significant revenue for the firm (note that it's generally only after your training that you really start to add value). And if you can't convince a firm of this, you're unlikely to succeed. So how do you demonstrate passion for the business? Well, this involves demonstrating your motivation for wanting to work in the industry (i.e. your "career motivation") and, more specifically, your motivation for wanting to work at the firm you're applying to (i.e. your "firm motivation"). Note that "Why do you want to pursue this career?" is often asked as a separate question to "Why do you want to work at this firm?", so don't mix them up, and make sure you prepare solid answers to both. Now the irony isn't lost on me that I quit the City right after my training. But during the recruitment process, I worked hard on articulating my motivations, and backed these up with solid research and experience.

Career motivation questions

Many candidates struggle to articulate their motivation for pursuing a particular career. However, this can be an incredibly important element of the recruitment process, so give your motivation some serious thought when preparing. Moreover, if there are various options for specialising as part of the career, make sure you can explain why you're interested in the specialism for which you're applying. For example, if you're pursuing a career in commercial law, make sure you're ready to explain not only why you want to be a lawyer, but also – more specifically – a *commercial* lawyer. You might even be questioned about which particular *area* of commercial law you're interested in, so make sure you know enough about the career to provide a more specific answer.

Examples of career motivation questions

When it comes to motivation questions, the first challenge is to convince a firm that you want to work within their industry, in the specific role you're applying for. In other words, you need to demonstrate your *career motivation*. To give context, I'll start by quickly going through some common examples of career motivation questions.

Q. What influenced your decision to pursue this particular career?

This is the question that most commonly arises, so I have covered it in detail throughout this section.

Q. Which other careers have you considered and why did you not want to pursue them instead?

This type of question is designed to test whether you have properly explored your options, which will be seen as a sensible approach when it comes to potentially defining the rest of your working life. It's absolutely fine to mention alternative careers (e.g. aspiring commercial lawyers could mention that they have considered a career as a barrister), as long as you're able to explain why you have a preference for the role you're currently applying to. On that note, be prepared for the interviewer to pick out previous unrelated positions, internships or experiences that you highlighted as part of your application, then ask why you didn't go down those specific routes. For instance, an aspiring commercial lawyer who has worked extensively at a university newspaper may be asked why they are choosing law over journalism.

Q. What is your understanding of the role for which you are applying?

This isn't a question that people necessarily give much thought to. However, how can you credibly claim that you want to carry out a role if you're unable to explain what the role will involve? Make sure you're able to deliver a solid answer to this question, as it's designed to assess whether you have truly done your research and thought about the career. And therefore whether your motivations are credible.

Q. Where do you see yourself in 10 years' time?

This question is designed to test whether you have thought about the career in the long-term, which can indicate whether you've carefully considered your motivation, and are likely to commit to the firm for the foreseeable future. You don't need to say you're 100% sure you'll want to remain in the career for a decade or more (if anything, this may come across a naïve). However, stating that you hope you will have progressed up the ranks to a certain position by that stage, within a department that you find particularly interesting – and that you'll be adding real value and excelling in your role – is probably a fair way of approaching your answer. Either way, when preparing an answer, don't forget to consider what "typical" progression actually looks like at the firm.

Structuring your answer

When discussing your career motivation, consider explaining the path that has led you to deciding to pursue a career in the relevant industry. Telling the story of how your interest developed can help your answer to seem more genuine, personal and credible. After all, nobody will believe you if you simply say that you've wanted to be a lawyer or banker since the age of 5! When doing this, you essentially want to cover: **how** you learned about the profession; **what** you learned, did and/or were exposed to; and **why** you found this appealing. In terms of a high-level structure, you could perhaps go through your experiences chronologically, covering the *how, what* and *why* for each experience. For example:

Step 1. How did your interest develop?

Perhaps start by identifying which experience sparked your initial interest in the career (either the specific role, or the industry more generally). For instance, when did your interest in your chosen career first materialise? Was it a conversation you had whilst at school? A particular school or university module? An insight you gained from a career fair? A particular stint of work experience?

Step 2. What did you learn?

Next, explain *what* you initially learned about the career. For example, you could highlight the aspects of the career that, through this experience, you realised align with your skills, interests and ambitions. Perhaps it was the nature of the work (including the intellectual challenge), as well as specific aspects of the role such as the client-facing elements and focus on teamwork?

Step 3. Why did this appeal?

You should then explain how what you learned helped to further your interest in the career. Draw out your motivations, and link these back to *you*. For example, *why* does the prospect of an intellectual challenge appeal? *Why* do you want to work in a client-facing environment? *Why* are you attracted to the prospect of working in teams? And so on. Note that we cover this in more detail in the next section.

Step 4. How did you explore this interest?

Once you have discussed how a particular experience furthered your interest in the career, highlight the next steps you actively took to continue exploring the career and developing your motivation. Doing so is key if you want to give real credibility to your answers. After all, the fact that you took these subsequent steps suggests you really did enjoy whatever it was you had previously experienced. Why else would you have continued to give up your free time to learn more about the career?

For example, did you decide to study your degree subject on this basis, or elect to study a related module as part of an unrelated degree (for example a philosophy student choosing to study a jurisprudence module to explore their interest in a legal career)? Did you attend career fairs and employer events, join relevant societies, carry out related volunteering roles, or apply for work experience (whether this involved work shadowing, insight days, internships or part-time work)? Or did you attend industry events, actively network with people who work in related roles, and read books or complete online courses designed to educate you about the career and industry? Then, as before, go on to explain what you learned and how these learnings furthered your interest in the career. In other words, continue to demonstrate how your research, exploration and experiences confirmed that this was the right career for you.

My interest in [career] stems from [first experience] → As a result of [first experience], I learned [insteresting aspect of the career] → [Interesting aspect] appealed because [give personal reasons] → As a result, [discuss next experience], where I learned... ... and so on

Drawing out your motivations

It's important that you distinguish between your career motivation (i.e. what you *want* to do) and your skills (i.e. what you're *good* at doing). Many candidates say things like "I want to be a lawyer because my skillset aligns with the career", but the former doesn't necessarily follow on from the latter. For example, I'm good at writing, a confident communicator and very well organised, which means I would probably make a very good administrative assistant. However, just because I possess these skills doesn't mean that, by default, I would *want* to carry out that role.

In addition, if you're linking previous work experiences to your motivation to become, for example, a lawyer or banker, don't focus solely (or predominantly) on what you *did* during those work experiences. It's less about what you did, and more about what you were exposed to and how you felt about it. The fact that you have carried out some basic legal work might demonstrate your competence (which could be helpful when answering a competency question). However, it doesn't in and of itself convey that you enjoyed the work and would like to continue doing such work throughout your career. By all means mention your previous work experiences and explain how these exposed you to certain aspects of the career. But don't then forget to explain how these aspects have cumulatively contributed to your desire to pursue your chosen career. And be sure to relate each motivating factor back to your personal experiences, ambitions and interests. I cannot stress this enough: it's a key feature that distinguishes distinctive, personal, credible answers from generic and unconvincing answers. So always explain *why* you care!

With this in mind, I'll now give examples of some of the aspects that you may want to consider when trying to convey your personal reasons for pursuing your chosen career (these examples are the types of points you might want to make in step 3 of the structure proposed in the previous section). Note that this list is by no means exhaustive – these are just a handful of examples to guide you – so it's imperative that you think about your own personal motivations so that you can then relate your answers back to yourself. Moreover, some of the considerations mentioned below relate to multiple careers, whilst others do not. It's fine to mention factors that relate to multiple careers (e.g. you want to work in a team, or in a client-facing role), as long as the selection of factors you choose to mention *cumulatively* point only to your chosen career path.

The career aligns with your interests

One reason for pursuing a career is that various aspects of that career align with your interests. It might be your interest in the business world, current affairs, the subject matter, the wider industry, or a combination of these. If this is the case, then explain what your interests are, how you developed them, and how each interest aligns with the role for which you are applying. To put this into context, I have included some examples in the blue box below.

Interest in the commercial world

Are you attracted to the business-centric nature of the career, or the opportunity to work with businesses throughout the various stages of their life cycles? Are you interested in carrying out work that could have a broad commercial impact on clients' businesses more generally? Or do you feel the career is at the intersection of a number of your interests (for example, commercial law is arguably at the intersection of business, finance, law and politics)? If so, explain how you developed your interest. Does your interest in business stem from growing up on the periphery of a family business, or from running your own side hustle? Or is your interest based on the fact that finance affects many aspects of everyday life, or that the law governs everything we do?

Academic interests

Does the opportunity to carry out work that involves the practical application of the concepts you have studied in an academic context appeal? If so, why? Did you particularly enjoy studying school subjects or university modules that relate to your chosen career (e.g. Economics, Business, Finance, or commercially-oriented Law modules such as Contract)? If you did, perhaps take your answer even further. You could explain why you enjoyed the subject matter from an academic standpoint, then elaborate on why you think utilising that knowledge will be even more interesting in practice.

Interest in the industry

Do you have a longstanding interest in the relevant industry? Do you want to work in an industry that's facing constant change and disruption? Or are you interested in the trajectory of the industry? If talking about the industry, explain how you learned about the industry, what you learned, and why you find it so interesting (note that this can also subtly demonstrate commercial awareness). Do you avidly read the commercial news or subscribe to industry newsletters? Do you feel that the constant change and disruption suggests your career will be dynamic and stimulating?

The nature of the work appeals

You could also consider the nature of the work you'll be carrying out on a day-to-day basis, as long as you take the time to explain why you feel that the nature of the work will personally appeal to you. You could also elaborate on why this suggests your career will be fulfilling in the longer-term. To put this into context, I have included some examples in the blue box below.

The intellectual challenge

Are you likely to carry out unique, interesting work that provides a constant intellectual challenge? Linked to this, will there be unrivalled opportunities to continue learning and developing, perhaps with a steep learning curve? If so, why do you care? Does the potentially challenging work suggest you will rarely find yourself clock-watching or feeling intellectually unfulfilled? If the learning curve appeals, can you give an example of where you have enjoyed a particularly steep learning curve in the past?

Day-to-day tasks

Does the work involve specific tasks that you believe you'll enjoy? For example, are you attracted to the prospect of problem solving on a daily basis, carrying out in-depth research, producing reports, delivering presentations, or contributing to the commercial decisions of large corporate clients? Do you particularly enjoy the challenge of identifying and mitigating risk, analysing the nuances of language, or processing vast amounts of data?

If so, link your statements back to your own experiences. Have you previously enjoyed carrying out similar tasks, for example during your studies or whilst undertaking extracurricular activities? Did you enjoy carrying out these tasks whilst participating in workshops designed to simulate the type of work in which the firm engages? If so, what specifically did you enjoy? The detail-oriented nature of the work?

The variety

Will you be exposed to a broad variety of work, and have the opportunity to work for a range of interesting, perhaps high-profile clients? Does this appeal because you've previously enjoyed roles where there has been real variety on offer? Does this suggest the career will remain stimulating in the long-term? If you want to work for high-profile clients, is this because you feel this work will be more interesting and rewarding?

The nature of the role appeals

You could also consider the role you're applying for more broadly. What does it involve? Who will you be working with? What is the day-to-day like? And so on. Just make sure you explain how you found out about the role and *why* certain aspects interest you.

Ways of working

Are you attracted to the prospect of working in a client-facing role, with a focus on building client relations? Do you want to work predominantly in teams? If so, explain why these aspects appeal. Have you worked in a client-facing role in the past, and if so, what did you like about it? The social aspect of building relationships with clients (aka customers)? The skill involved in dealing with different types of people? Why do you prefer working in teams rather than independently? Have you thrived in the past when working collaboratively with others, perhaps at university or as a member of a club?

The working environment

Do you think you'll thrive in a highly pressurised environment? If so, how can you back this up? Have you particularly enjoyed working in a similar environment in the past (e.g. spending long hours undertaking challenging work), for example when working on group projects or undertaking work experience? If you have, why did you enjoy it? Did the pressure keep you absorbed and engaged? Does this suggest the career will remain fulfilling? If you have not accumulated such experiences, have you experienced the opposite type of working environment, with no stress, few working hours and little intellectual engagement? If so, did this make you realise that you would prefer to work in a more pressurised or dynamic environment? To give a personal example, I had taken on a variety of jobs throughout my education, including a paper round, a job pushing trolleys in a supermarket and a job lifting wooden planks up staircases on a building site. I compared these experiences to my chosen career, explaining that although my previous jobs typically involved favourable working hours and little stress, I had not felt intellectually engaged, or that there were opportunities to significantly develop my personal skills and capabilities. This meant that I lacked a sense of personal fulfilment and achievement, which is why I wanted instead to pursue an intellectually challenging career and work in a dynamic and pressurised working environment.

Working in an international context

If you are interviewing at an international firm, you should also consider explaining why the international element of the career appeals. Do you have a real interest in working on cross-border matters, potentially for high profile global corporations? If so, how can you back this up? Have you chosen to study abroad, attend international study programmes, travel, or learn other languages? If not, do you simply feel that the opportunity to engage in complex, cross-border transactions will provide the greatest possible intellectual challenge? Or does the prospect of working with other employees and clients from a variety of countries and cultures indicate your career will remain interesting and varied? To substantiate such a claim, you could relay any positive past experiences you may have had when working in a team with people from a variety of different backgrounds.

To summarise, make sure you support your statements by providing personal examples to illustrate that certain aspects of the career *genuinely* appeal. Tie everything back to your personal experiences, ambitions and interests!

> **Practical tip:** discussing other careers that you have considered can help to validate your answers (although this might be more appropriate in an interview, as you're not limited by word count). If you have explored alternative careers, perhaps explain how those other experiences have helped to confirm what you really want from your career. As part of this, you could mention the elements of those potential careers that appealed less, and highlight the aspects of your chosen career that appeal to a greater degree. For instance, if you decide you want to be a commercial lawyer but have previously undertaken an investment banking internship, explain what you liked less about investment banking (perhaps the focus on numbers?), and then explain the elements of a career in commercial law that appeal more (perhaps the focus on language?). If instead you were explaining why you would rather be a solicitor than a barrister, you could mention that solicitors tend to work more in teams, barristers don't generally work on transactional matters, solicitors might have the opportunity to carry out a variety of work for a client throughout its business journey, whereas barristers only tend to be brought in when something goes wrong, and so on.

A worked example

To put this all into context, here's an example of how I could discuss my own motivation for pursuing a career in law, based on my chronological journey. I would start by explaining that my interest in a legal career stemmed from my experience being talked through a recording contract back in my days as a musician. During that experience, I remember thinking that I would enjoy working in a client-facing role that involved explaining complex concepts to people like myself, and I was interested in how various risks had been anticipated and mitigated in the recording contract. As a result, I carried out work experience at the firm, where I gained more of an insight into the sheer variety of legal work on offer, as well as the commercial nature of the work and the focus on language. This very much appealed, as I had always enjoyed studying the nuances of language during my A-levels and as a lyricist, which led to me studying Law & Business at university. During my degree, I particularly enjoyed the business focus of the more commercial legal modules, as well as the problem-solving aspects of practically applying the law (something that I knew was an inherent part of the role of commercial lawyers). Consequently, I attended dozens of open days and employer presentations, each of which furthered my interest in commercial law. In particular, I learned about the international elements of the work carried out by City law firms, as well as the diverse range of high-profile clients serviced and the focus on working in teams. This resonated, as I had a genuine interest in working on cross-border matters for large multinationals, as I felt this work would be the most intellectually engaging, and had always enjoyed working collaboratively with others towards a common goal. And that's a wrap.

Firm motivation questions

Once you've convinced a firm that you want to work within their industry, the next challenge is to convince them that there's nowhere else you would rather train. Now, I know that researching firms and differentiating them from competitors can be an onerous task, but you must remember that there are fewer roles available than the number of people good enough to successfully take on those roles. For this reason, it's incredibly important that you carry out high quality research into each firm so that you can properly articulate your reasons for wanting to work there. If you receive two or three rejections for answering "why this firm?" too generically, odds are you would receive another fifty rejections if you simply tried to hedge your bets by applying to more firms. This is one of the reasons why you tend see candidates receiving either no offers or multiple offers. By all means apply to 10 or 11 firms, but only if you have the time to undertake sufficient research in order to ensure your answers are not too generic. In addition, firm research can help you to ascertain which *type* of firm you *actually* want to work for. And this is important, as you'll likely be happier in your career if you work for a firm whose clients, work and culture align with your interests, skills and values.

Examples of firm motivation questions

Q. Why do you want to work for this firm?

Firms will generally expect you to differentiate them from their competitors, which will typically require ample research. As this is the question that most commonly arises, I have covered it in detail throughout this section.

Q. Which other firms have you applied to and why do you prefer this firm?

You may well be asked which other firms you have applied to, and it's absolutely fine to mention the firm's competitors. In fact, *not* mentioning a firm's competitors might suggest that your career motivation is a little uncertain. For example, if you're applying to a large international City law firm or a global investment bank and you say that all the other firms you've applied to are boutique, regional firms, this might suggest that you don't yet really know what you want from your career (in turn suggesting you are a risky choice for the firm to make...more of a flight risk).

Also be prepared to justify why you have applied to these other firms and to explain why the present firm is your first choice. Of course, it's not a problem if you're still exploring your options (or hedging your bets) by applying to a range of different types of firms for work experience or internships. Just carefully consider which firms you *mention* if you're asked this question, be prepared to justify why you have applied to those other firms, and be ready to explain why the present firm is your first choice.

Q. Talk about a particular deal the firm has been involved in and why you found it interesting.

This type of question is designed to test whether you have researched the firm in detail. I received this question in multiple interviews, so it's definitely worth having to hand a couple of examples of the firm's recent work.

Q. How does the firm remain competitive?

This type of question relates more to the firm's offering to clients than its offering to employees, and again is testing whether you've researched the firm in detail (as well as your knowledge of how firms operate as businesses). Your answer might cover aspects such as the firm's experience, capabilities, global reach, ability to build relationships with clients, track record of innovating, ability to attract and retain talent, and so on. There will likely be overlap with what you would discuss if asked why you want to work for the firm, but you would certainly need to tweak your approach.

Drawing out your firm motivations

When carrying out firm research and articulating your answers to firm motivation questions (or the "why the firm" section of a cover letter), don't focus on fairly generic attributes and insights that merely reflect a quick skim of the firm's website and marketing materials. Instead, try to identify features that genuinely and convincingly distinguish the firm (note that it's fine to mention certain features that apply to a few other firms, as long as the *selection of factors* you highlight cumulatively point only to the relevant firm). Once you've done this, then relate these elements back to *you*. Tell the firm *why* you care. *Why* the selling points you have highlighted genuinely appeal. *Why* they align with or link to your interests, motivations, ambitions and/or previous experiences. *Why* they will, together, provide a *better training experience* than the firm's competitors are able to offer.

Now, this last part is important, but people often lose sight of it. Whilst it might make sense to discuss the firm's culture, values, reputation and approach to training – as these factors are likely to have an impact on *your day-to-day* experience from the outset – it often wouldn't make sense to discuss a firm's revenue or profitability, as this most likely won't impact you as a junior (assuming you're not being offered an ownership stake in the business!). With this in mind, below are some of the factors that you may want to keep in mind when considering your personal reasons for applying to a particular firm. Note that these are just a handful of examples to guide you. This list is by no means exhaustive, so it's imperative that you carry out thorough research and reflect upon your personal motivations so that you can relate the firm's (ideally unique) selling points back to yourself.

Reputation and capabilities

It's fine to mention that you are attracted to a firm as a result of its reputation, the awards it has received, the sectors it services, the work it carries out, and the types of clients it attracts. However, don't linger on these points for too long if you're not able to identify factors that *truly* distinguish the firm from most (or all) of its competitors. This can be a real challenge, as most of the firm's competitors will probably have a similar reputation, have won similar awards, service predominantly the same sectors, carry out very similar work (remember, firms will often be on opposite sides of the same deals and cases), and work for many of the same clients (large clients typically have multiple law firms on a "panel" and delegate work to different firms on this panel at different times, meaning many firms *literally* have the same clients).

If you do manage to identify something about the firm's reputation that is unique or particularly relevant to you, be sure to explain this clearly. What is it about that selling point you've highlighted that aligns with your skills, interests, experiences and/or motivations? To put this into context, I have included some examples in the blue box below.

Rankings and awards

- Is the firm highly ranked across a *broader range of departments or practice areas* than most of its competitors? For example, not just corporate and finance (which many firms might demonstrate strength in), but also real estate, disputes and intellectual property? Has it won awards to back this up? Does it have a leading reputation in the areas that interest you most? As well as corporate expertise, does the firm also exhibit strength in teams that are likely to remain busy during economic downturns (for example, teams that work on restructurings or disputes).

- **Explain why you care:** could strength across a broad range of departments suggest you'll have consistent exposure to pioneering work wherever you are placed during your training, as well as the opportunity to learn from the best in their fields? If so, does this reflect positively on your potential to learn and develop during the firm's training programme? Or do you have a demonstrable interest in a particular practice area for which the firm is ranked "Band 1" by Chambers and Partners, and are you therefore attracted to the opportunity to join such a highly regarded team and carry out such high-profile work? If a firm exhibits strength in teams that are likely to remain busy during times of economic uncertainty, could this reflect positively on your future job security?

Groundbreaking work

- Has the firm worked on a particularly unique, groundbreaking or interesting matter? For example, has it advised on a global sporting event (e.g. the Olympics), the largest acquisition of the year, a particularly high-profile dispute, or the launch of a new pioneering product from a high-profile technology company? To give an example, on my Freshfields application, I mentioned the firm's work on the London 2012 Olympics, as this was such a unique and high-profile mandate, the firm's role was so broad and interesting, and Freshfields was apparently the *only* law firm mandated to work on the event.

- **Explain why you care:** explain why you found the matter so interesting, and why this example suggests you will have a better training experience. For example, does it suggest you would have consistent exposure to equally as interesting, high-profile or cutting-edge work as a junior? If so, could this better facilitate your professional development from the outset? Going back to the Olympics example, I explained that this work aligned with my interest in sport, and hypothesised that if the firm was able to beat its competitors to win such an amazing project, this suggested I could be working on similarly interesting projects if I were to secure a training contract (I might have even mentioned future world cups as an example).

- **Tip:** if you do mention the firm's work, make sure that you can talk about it in some detail. For example, why did the firm's client proceed with a particular acquisition? Was it successful? What was important about the deal? Were there any (publicly known) challenges?

Unique sector focus and/or client base

- Does the firm work with specific types of clients – or carry out work in specific sectors – that differentiates it from most competitors? For example, whilst many large professional services firms might carry out corporate and finance-related work for large corporations, some might also work with sporting, gaming, media or shipping clients, or carry out work for earlier stage businesses.

- **Explain why you care:** do you have a particular interest in the more unique or niche clients and sectors serviced by the firm? If so, explain how you developed this interest. For example, does your education demonstrate a corresponding interest in the sectors you want to highlight, or have you worked in the sector or for similar types of clients in the past? To give an example, I once worked with a student who applied mainly to firms with leading shipping practices, and focused part of her firm motivation answers on the prowess of their shipping teams. She then linked this sector focus to her own keen interest in shipping, which was clearly demonstrated by the fact that she studied a master's degree in shipping law and had completed various shipping qualifications in her spare time.

- **Tip:** if you bring up a client or sector, questions on that client or sector are fair game. if you plan to discuss clients, make sure you can name a few that support your point, and try to find examples of the work the firm has carried out for those clients. If discussing sectors, be prepared to talk about the work carried out in relation to those sectors, and perhaps also look into the trends affecting those sectors more generally.

International footprint and expansion

Discussing a firm's international reach can often veer into the generic, so be careful with this one. Most large City firms have offices in (or operate in) many of the same jurisdictions, so it can be difficult to identify specific factors that are convincing differentiators. Moreover, you should never talk about a firm as if it is a travel agency; travel opportunities vary between firms and industries and can be few and far between for juniors, so focusing on your desire to travel may not suggest your motivations are particularly relevant. However, I have included some examples in the blue box below that might be worth considering in limited circumstances.

International experience

- Has the firm been the undisputable leader in a particular jurisdiction for a number of years? Has it won a series of high-profile awards in recognition of its work in a particular country? Does it work more with emerging markets than other firms? Or has it worked on a groundbreaking international deal, perhaps with dozens of jurisdictions involved or a tangible social impact?

- **Explain why you care:** if you mention these types of points, highlight why you are particularly interested in the jurisdiction you choose to highlight. For example, have you previously worked or lived there?

- **Tip:** be sure to check that the specific office you are applying to join actually works on matters involving the jurisdictions you mention, otherwise it may be a moot point. For example, if you're applying to the London office, and you have a personal interest in Latin America that you want to link to the firm's work involving that region, make sure there are actually opportunities to get involved in that work from the London office.

International footprint

- Does the firm have a greater spread of international offices than its competitors? Does it have offices in particularly unique jurisdictions? Is the firm uniquely strong across multiple key jurisdictions, perhaps following mergers with leading firms that were headquartered in those jurisdictions? Or does the firm have a particularly unique approach to international work, for example by collaborating with a network of third party "best friend" firms who are leaders in their jurisdictions?

- **Explain why you care:** could working within a global network of offices offer opportunities to benefit from the knowledge, insights and expertise of others from all over the world? Could a firm's presence across multiple jurisdictions mean it's better placed to win the most complex cross-border mandates, thus giving you the chance to work on a uniquely interesting range of challenging matters? Might there be more opportunities to work abroad if the firm has a comprehensive global footprint? Would a "best friends" approach to international work appeal more? Could this approach provide the opportunity to work with and learn from some of the most highly regarded professionals from leading firms around the world? More generally, do these aspects align with your international mindset? If so, explain how you developed this international mindset. For example, was it through growing up, studying or working in different countries, and/or learning multiple languages

> 📖 **International mindset:** although the phrase has no objective definition, I understand "international mindset" to mean having a desire and ability to absorb, appreciate and adjust to different environments, markets and cultures, which can enhance your ability to effectively (and professionally) communicate and collaborate with people from around the world.

Growth and expansion

- Was the firm the first in the market to open offices in a new and exciting emerging market? Is the firm currently in an exciting stage of growth more generally? Has the firm opened offices that will help it to win more work in a specific sector or from a certain category of client (e.g. has it expanded into one or more technology hubs to enhance its reputation for carrying out cutting-edge technology work)? Or has the firm expanded to compete with other firms and protect its competitive advantage? For example, a UK-headquartered firm might expand into the US to ensure it has the same cross-border capabilities as US-headquartered firms that have already expanded into the UK.

- **Explain why you care:** did the firm's decision to open a particular office demonstrate its desire to grow and excel in an area that particularly interests you? If so, *why* does this area interest you? Do the openings of new offices demonstrate that the firm is agile, forward-thinking and opportunistic? Does this indicate that the firm will maintain its leading position, or become a market leader? Would it be exciting to join during a period of significant growth and evolution?

- **Tip:** note that if you choose to discuss a firm's international expansion, you may well be asked to recommend where else the firm should open an office, so give this some thought in advance!

Headquarters

- If the firm is headquartered in a different jurisdiction, see if you can differentiate it from other firms headquartered in the same jurisdiction, as well as firms in the jurisdiction where you are applying. For example, if you are applying to the London office of a US-headquartered firm, does that firm have a greater presence in London than any US competitors, but a better reputation and client base in the US than any London-headquartered firms?

- **Explain why you care:** could this suggest the firm is better placed to win work that straddles those jurisdictions, and if so, can you demonstrate why you're particularly interested in such work? Or might this indicate that the firm has a better chance of attracting high-profile clients that are headquartered in the same place? Remember, those clients may well have work that needs to be carried out in London one day!

Training and development

When it comes to training, most firms have at least one distinguishing feature, for example shorter rotations between teams, better international secondment opportunities (or even guaranteed secondment opportunities), specialist learning and development programmes, smaller trainee or analyst intakes, and the like. I have included some more detailed examples below.

Structure of the training

- Does the firm's training programme enable you to experience a *broader range* of departments than its competitors' training programmes, for example by allowing shorter rotations between departments? Or does the firm offer seats across a greater variety of teams? Alternatively, does the firm guarantee you a seat in the practice area that most interests you? Note that firms have different policies regarding "mandatory" seats. Some firms might require all trainees to spend at least one seat in a specific team – often corporate, finance or disputes – whereas others might designate two or three mandatory seats (or require you to choose two out of three options).

- **Explain why you care:** if a firm's approach is distinctively flexible (or offers more variety), does this mean you'll be able to experience a greater range of work? If so, will this increase your chances of identifying the type of work that best aligns with your skills and interests, and therefore help you to make a more informed decision about where to qualify or specialise post-training? Could experiencing more areas also give you a uniquely holistic insight into how various aspects of matters fit together, and in doing so, further your commercial awareness and broader professional development? These are some of the points I drew out on my Freshfields application, as the firm offered 3-month seats (in contrast to the 6-month rotations offered by most competitors). Whether you see mandatory seats as a pro or a con will depend somewhat on whether your interests align with the designated practice area(s). If your interests do align, then explain this. You might feel that one mandatory seat constitutes a selling point, as it strikes a balance between flexibility and guaranteeing your exposure to a specific team (provided you're actually interested in that team). You could even refer to a "mandatory" seat as a "guaranteed" seat, as this puts a more positive spin on the requirement.

Approach to training

- Is the firm more focused on classroom-based learning at the start, or does it prefer to give juniors practical, client-facing experience from the outset? Are you afforded greater opportunities to develop your technical and business knowledge and/or professional skills during your training? For example, are you applying to a law firm that offers not only the usual legal training, but also runs some kind of academy that provides opportunities to develop business knowledge (e.g. through attending client-led seminars) and soft skills (e.g. through expert-led workshops)? Alternatively, are employees encouraged to get involved in business development initiatives or to bring in work? Or does the firm offer grants to help you pay for language courses or additional qualifications, for example the Chartered Financial Analyst (CFA) qualification or a Master of Business Administration (MBA)?

- **Explain why you care:** if you are attracted to a firm because it promises practical experience and ample exposure to clients, then explain why this matters, perhaps linking back to experiences where you have enjoyed (and thrived while) learning by doing. Could a more holistic approach to training – one that creates opportunities to develop not just the technical knowledge you need as a junior, but also broader business and professional skills – potentially help you to emerge as a more well-rounded professional? If so, will this better prepare you for a more senior role?

Support and supervision

- What kind of supervision and support are you provided throughout? Do you have dedicated mentors (perhaps at various levels of seniority), regular supervisor catch-ups and frequent appraisals? Are there regular technical training sessions within each team, as well as frequent trainee-specific seminars? What about e-learning resources that you can access on demand? Has the firm brought in particular measures more recently to support employees in light of changes to the working environment (e.g. initiatives designed to mitigate potentially negative impacts of remote working)?

- **Explain why you care:** does the firm's approach to developing its employees align with your preferred means of learning and developing? If so, perhaps explain how you discovered that this approach works best for you. If you will be allocated buddies or mentors at varying levels of seniority, could this enable you to learn from and build relationships with a broad range of professionals? If the firm is constantly adapting its approach to training employees, does this suggest you would be consistently and effectively supported in your role?

Size of intake and teams

- Does the firm hire only a small intake of juniors each year, or would you be part of a large pool of newbies? Does the firm tend to staff smaller teams on matters (e.g. staffing a partner, one or two associates, and a trainee on deals), or much larger teams?

- **Explain why you care:** link your comments about intake and team size to your preferred working style. For example, you might prefer being part of a smaller intake or working in smaller teams if you feel this would give you the chance to earn greater responsibility and exposure at an earlier stage (perhaps because fewer juniors tend to be staffed on matters in firms with smaller intakes and teams). You might also feel less anonymous and more integral when working as part of a smaller team. Conversely, you might prefer the idea of joining a larger intake or working in larger teams, as this could give you a larger pool of colleagues with whom you can form professional relationships and from who you can learn.

Secondments and placements

- Does the firm offer unparalleled or particularly unique opportunities to work in overseas offices or go on international, client or pro bono secondments during your training programme? Note that simply stating that a firm offers international opportunities likely won't differentiate the firm from its closest competitors. However, if the firm is *one of the only* firms to offer (for example) *guaranteed* secondments, pro bono secondments, or stints at particularly interesting clients' offices, or if the firm offers a *greater range* of international secondments than its competitors, then this might be a sufficiently unique point to raise.

- **Explain why you care:** do international secondments appeal because you have a genuine interest in working internationally and building relationships with colleagues around the world? If so, be prepared to explain how you have explored this interest to date, which jurisdictions you would like to work in, and why. Do you feel that international placements would be enriching experiences that can provide an awareness of cultural and regional differences? Is this especially important given how much of the firm's work is multi-jurisdictional? Do client secondments appeal because they would enable you to better understand clients' perspectives and priorities, and how they operate more generally (including how they make decisions)? Could this hone your commercial acumen by shaping your understanding of how different companies operate from a commercial standpoint, thus feeding into your broader professional development?

Longer term development

- Are you expected to specialise soon after you qualify, or does the firm encourage you to develop a broader practice? For example, if you decide to qualify as a finance lawyer, will you have the opportunity to work on a broad range of finance-related matters (e.g. corporate lending, acquisition finance, real estate finance, debt capital markets, restructuring etc.), or will you be expected to pursue a narrower sub-category of finance work?

- **Explain why you care:** do you feel that specialising in a niche area will enable you to develop deep technical expertise and truly get to grips with that area from an earlier stage? Alternatively, if the firm enables its employees to carry out a broader range of work, will this help to ensure your career remains more varied and interesting, whilst providing more opportunities to learn in the long term. Or do you feel that building a broader base of experience will make you a more well-rounded professional?

People and culture

One of the easiest ways to differentiate City firms – many of which have similar clients, practices, global networks and training programmes – is by discussing their people and culture. In fact, many firms claim that their culture is their defining feature. Making generic, sweeping, unsupported statements about a firm's culture won't help your answer to stand out. However, if you take the time to explain how you gained an insight into the firm's people, working environment and culture more generally, and why this contributed to your motivation to work for the firm, you'll hopefully be delivering an answer that comes across as genuine, personal and well-researched.

You can learn about a firm's culture by meeting its people, for example during campus presentations, career fairs, open days or networking events. If you are unable to meet one of the firm's employees before applying, try to find out about the culture from other sources. Ask people at your university that have completed vacation schemes there, contact LinkedIn connections that have experienced or worked at the firm, or try to attend webinars or virtual insight days where firm employees will be presenting and answering questions (you could even check the firm's website for employee video interviews about the firm's culture). You may also have access to university lecturers or career advisers who used to work in industry (alternatively, they may be able to connect you with others who work in industry). Think outside the box. And as always, once you present your insights, don't forget to explain *why* the culture resonates with you. The blue box below gives more specific examples.

The people

- Have your previous interactions suggested that you would be working with bright, ambitious, like-minded people on a daily basis? Have you already met a truly diverse range of interesting employees? If so, perhaps mention who you met, where you met them, why you liked them, and what they said about the firm's culture. If you haven't spoken to anyone directly, did you read articles, watch videos, or see posts on social media that reflected positively on the firm's people?

- **Explain why you care:** have you enjoyed working with similar types of people in the past? Do you particularly value working as part of a diverse workforce? Perhaps a workforce where your own background and culture are represented? Did your interactions give the impression that you would fit into the firm's culture on both a professional and a social level? If so, why? Ultimately, explain how your interactions and conversations with employees impacted upon your perception of the firm.

- **Tip:** unless you're told otherwise, it's usually fine to mention the name and role of a firm representative with whom you've interacted (I was always flattered when people did this!). In fact, retaining this information can go some way to demonstrating how engaged you were when interacting with the firm. You could perhaps bring everything together by saying something to the effect of "The firm's [*quote about culture*] culture appeals, as explained by [*name and role of individual*] at [*event*], because [*give your reasons*].".

The working environment

- Does the firm purport to have a welcoming, supportive and non-hierarchal culture? Or is there something else about the working environment that appeals? Are you joining a large office with great facilities? Or a smaller office with a tight-knit team? Either way, if you mention the working environment, be sure to highlight how (or from who) you learned about it.

- **Explain why you care:** do you feel you are most likely to succeed in such a working environment? Or can you give an example of when you have previously enjoyed working in a firm or team that fostered a similar culture? Does a larger office indicate you will have access to a huge network of support? Or does a smaller office suggest you'll be less anonymous and have a more perceivable impact?

- **Tip:** if you have personally spent time at the firm and experienced its working environment, mention this and what you enjoyed about it. However, if you take this approach, be ready to talk about your experience in detail, including any work you might have got involved in. Note that you don't have to use examples from a professional setting to demonstrate that you enjoyed or thrived whilst working in a particular environment. For example, you might have realised that you like working in big (or small) teams, in supportive environments, or in more independent roles whilst volunteering, taking on a position of responsibility, or participating in an extra-curricular activity.

Social opportunities

- Does the firm offer a unique range of social activities and initiatives that align with your interests, for example sports clubs, music ensembles, book clubs, employee networks, pro bono initiatives, networking events and so on? I wouldn't focus on this too much (after all, the firm is primarily a *business*), but mentioning social opportunities can help to show your research. It can also demonstrate your interest in getting involved in the wider activities on offer at the firm, and therefore your interest in contributing positively to the firm's culture.

- **Explain why you care:** does the firm's investment in social activities and initiatives indicate that you will have ample opportunities to build stronger relationships with colleagues (outside the usual hierarchical constraints of the firm), contribute to the firm's culture, pursue your passions, and have some fun whilst working?

Retention rates

- Does the firm usually retain a high proportion of its trainees or analysts at the end of its training programme?

- **Explain why you care:** does a high retention rate indicate that trainees tend to develop a sufficiently impressive skill set and knowledge base throughout their training contracts to be kept on? Does it also evidence loyalty among juniors? Is all this a testament to the firm's ability to effectively train and support its juniors?

- **Tip:** if you discuss the support provided by a firm as part of a broader point about the firm's retention rates, this could provide another opportunity to show your research by mentioning some of the firm's specific training programmes and support-related initiatives. Interweaving selling points in this way can help to demonstrate that you have reflected holistically on the firm's offering (although make sure your structure remains strong and clear throughout).

Values, diversity and inclusion, charitable initiatives and corporate social responsibility

Firms generally place a great degree of importance on their values, commitments to diversity and inclusion, and investments in corporate social responsibility initiatives. Discussing these factors can help you to demonstrate that you will be a good cultural fit, that your values align with the firm's, and that you have a desire to contribute to the greater good. You can learn about a firm's values, diversity and inclusion initiatives, and corporate social responsibility programmes through discussions with its employees and other people who have previously interacted with the firm. Many firms also provide detailed information about these commitments on their websites and in their marketing materials.

Values

- Has the firm highlighted particular core values that it tries to instil in all employees? If so, has the firm demonstrated success in upholding these values? If you mention this, give examples.

- **Explain why you care:** do the firm's values align with your own, and if so, can you draw on previous experiences to evidence where you have previously demonstrated or upheld these values?

- **Tip:** if you mention values, make sure you understand what each value means (firms might have very specific explanations of what each of their values means), and be prepared to discuss them in detail.

Diversity and inclusion

- Does the firm take active steps to foster diversity and an inclusive working environment? Are there tangible examples to draw on that are unique to the firm, such as support networks for different demographics, or programmes designed to ensure anybody can reach the top regardless of (for example) background, gender, sexuality or culture? Has the firm taken a more proactive approach to inclusion following global events (e.g. COVID-19) and movements (e.g. the Black Lives Matter movement)? If so, mention any relevant initiatives, and be prepared to talk about what they involve.

- **Explain why you care:** for example, do you come from an underrepresented background and feel that the firm has demonstrated its success in supporting others from a similar background? Do you feel you are properly represented in the firm's workforce? Do you want to work in diverse teams? Do you feel inclusive environments foster greater team contributions and better learning opportunities? Whatever you say, be sure to explain the reasons behind the statements you make.

Corporate social responsibility

- Has the firm demonstrated a commitment to operating in a socially responsible manner? For example, has it been awarded B Corp status, or has it put in place initiatives to help it to operate more sustainability (e.g. has it set ambitious targets to reduce emissions, decided to go predominantly paperless, or switched to renewable energy sources)?

- **Explain why you care:** does this appeal because you're passionate about social welfare or sustainability, and want to work for a firm that shares your passion and upholds your standards?

Charitable initiatives and pro bono

- Does the firm invest time and money in certain causes that particularly resonate with you? For example, does the firm advise interesting social enterprises for free, donate to worthy charities, or support great causes that positively impact the local community? Or does the firm actively encourage its employees to commit to charitable initiatives, for example by tying their bonuses to the contribution of a certain minimum number of pro bono hours each year?

- **Explain why you care:** if there is a clear link between causes to which the firm commits, and causes that you have previously supported, draw this out. Perhaps you previously volunteered to support a certain cause and the firm would empower you to continue this work in some way? Or do you think the opportunity to get involved in substantive pro bono work will add another dimension to your development as a lawyer, through enabling you to build a broader skill set, gain unique perspectives, and consequently emerge as a more well-rounded individual?

- **Tip:** whilst volunteering may be worth mentioning, never forget that (most) firms are ultimately businesses that are primarily hiring you to help them make money, and that there are no guarantees that you'll have the capacity to contribute extensively to non-business activities. With this in mind, perhaps don't place a disproportionate amount of focus on volunteering.

Investment in technology and track record of innovation

Nowadays, innovation and technology play an essential part in ensuring firms can operate efficiently and effectively. Integrating technology such as automation into business processes can help firms to reduce costs, better utilise human capital, ensure greater compliance, produce more consistent output, and more. This has led to a significant investment in developing and/or adopting technology to help improve the ways in which professional services are delivered. And because some firms do this better than others, a firm's investment in technology and track record of innovating might contribute to your firm motivation.

Automation

- Has the firm invested heavily in technology designed to automate certain internal processes? More so than many of its competitors? If so, show your research by mentioning some of the technology developed or adopted and explaining its impact. Perhaps also look for examples of clients praising the firm's progress in this area, or of the firm winning work in part because of its investment in technology.

- **Explain why you care:** does the firm's investment in technology indicate that it wants to remain at the cutting-edge of innovation? If this helps it to operate more efficiently and cost-effectively, could this place the firm in a stronger position when it comes to pitching for work, given that clients are increasingly seeking more efficient and cost-effective professional services? If the firm is consequently able to win more market-leading mandates, does this indicate you'll have constant exposure to cutting-edge, intellectually challenging work? Alternatively, do you have a demonstrable interest in technology (perhaps you have studied technology-related courses, or you code in your spare time) which has led to you wanting to work in a firm that effectively integrates technology into its processes? Moreover, if technology has been adopted to automate some of the more administrative or labour-intensive legal processes, does this mean that juniors can focus on more substantive work, and therefore develop more quickly? Be careful with this last point however, as you don't want to come across as unwilling to get stuck in to the more mundane work!

- **Tip:** remember that automation isn't there to replace the substantive decision-making, analytical and problem-solving aspects of legal work. Clients still very much rely on human skill and experience to help tackle their tougher challenges and facilitate their business needs in practical and innovative ways, so don't talk about automation in a way that loses sight of this. After all, law firms are people-centric businesses, and it is *human* capital that enables firms to truly stand out (and for which firms can charge a great deal!). As a generalisation, automation is more about making administrative, repetitive and labour-intensive processes more efficient, cost-effective and/or consistent.

Innovation

- Does the firm do anything particularly unique in relation to innovation? For example, does it run its own incubator, develop its own software, get involved in technology conferences and so on? If mentioning this, be specific.

- **Explain why you care:** if there are opportunities to get involved in innovation-related initiatives, could this ensure you gain a broader base of experience as a junior, as well as the chance to develop skills that you will likely need in the future? For example, are there opportunities to undertake a placement in the firm's incubator, or to represent the firm at a conference? Does the firm crowdsource ideas for innovation from its employees and let employees contribute to the development of those ideas? Will this provide a more varied and interesting experience?

To conclude, I want to reiterate that you should not simply recite the phrases set out above. I have included these examples to give you a steer, but you'll ultimately need to carry out your own research and focus on the selling points that actually resonate with you. Otherwise you probably won't come across as convincing (and even if you get away with it on an application form, you may well be found out during an interview). Do your research. Give specific examples. And support your statements by linking them back to your wants, needs, experiences and motivations.

Research

Online resources

You can access information on industries and firms through a number of sources. For firms in particular, you could start with the firm's website, its annual report, articles it has published, press announcements and its profile on other websites (e.g. CommercialLaw.Academy, Prospects.ac.uk, TargetJobs.co.uk etc.), which can help you to learn about the firm's key differentiators and keep up to date with firm news, for example news relating to deals, poignant developments, awards and expansion plans. You could also follow the firm's social media channels (including LinkedIn) and sources such as The Lawyer and The Financial Times. However (and this cannot be reiterated enough!), be wary of regurgitating this information without explaining why certain aspects of the firm particularly appeal to you. It is likely that the graduate recruitment team wrote at least some of the content on these research sources, so simply reproducing the information could give the impression that your research was shallow.

Firm and industry events

Speaking to firms' employees during campus presentations, career fairs, office visits and networking events could give you a better insight into the industry, as well as the firm's culture and the day-to-day life of an employee. The same goes for firm-led webinars, virtual insight days or even interviews with employees on firm websites. Some of the information you come across may be less accessible to other candidates, so could help to set you apart when answering motivation questions. University societies may also provide unique opportunities to gain insights into industries and meet with firm representatives, so join relevant societies and get involved! Note that you may have to sign up for these types of events in advance, so check whether this is the case.

Consider requesting the email addresses of the people you talk to, or connecting with them on LinkedIn after an event. You can then reach out to thank them again for their time (and remind them who you are), and perhaps even swing another call or meeting to enable you to pick up additional insights into life at the firm. However, don't be too pushy, as these people are generally very busy. If you have created a strong first impression, this could also potentially help you to progress through to the interview stage, as some firms tend to flag impressive candidates on their system after meeting them in person. In that regard, I benefitted enormously from meeting a variety of firms (and their employees) at countless campus presentations, career fairs and office visits during my time at university. Note that some firms make a note of who attends their events, so if you plan on claiming that you were at a particular presentation, make sure that you actually went!

> **Practical tip:** when speaking to employees, always have a pen and paper to hand, and take notes! You may not interview at that firm for another year and a half, so will likely otherwise forget all the insights you have worked so hard to pick up.

Your network

Last, but by no means least, use your network. If there are students at your university that have already interned at a firm, or you have LinkedIn connections, friends, family members, careers advisers or university lecturers that have worked in the industry (or even better, worked for the firm), approach them and ask if they'll talk to you about their personal experiences over coffee. Then be sure to work on building relationships with those you meet. For example, if a contact gives you some guidance and you subsequently secure an internship or job offer, message them to thank them and keep them informed. Similarly if you find out that someone at your university has secured an internship or a graduate job at the same firm as you, get in touch before you start work in order to start building that relationship at the earliest stage possible.

Law firm research, profiles and interview insights

 148 lessons

1.5 hours of video content

Commercial Awareness

Commercial awareness is generally one of the most feared aspects of an interview process. However, this tends to be more because applicants don't really understand what is meant by commercial awareness, which can make it very difficult to prepare. This chapter aims to clarify what is meant by commercial awareness, how it can come up in interviews and how you can prepare.

Introduction to commercial awareness

What is "commercial awareness"?

To broadly summarise, if a person is "commercially aware", this means they have at least a foundational understanding of how businesses operate, as well as a general awareness of the broader economic, political and commercial factors that can affect businesses and the industries in which they operate. This could include an understanding of the types of strategies that businesses pursue (for example, an understanding of why and how businesses raise finance or engage in M&A activity) and the risks and threats that businesses face. It can also include knowledge of current affairs, industry trends, political events and the economy, as well as a foundational understanding of how these factors can affect firms and their clients.

Why is commercial awareness important?

Commercial awareness helps advisers to understand their clients, including those clients' businesses, their priorities, their competitors and their industries. It involves having the ability to consider not only the legal, commercial and financial issues that affect clients, but also the potential commercial impact of the economic climate, political environment, industry trends and other developments that affect clients' industries more broadly. This can all help advisers to provide informed, contextual advice that maximises clients' opportunities and minimises their exposure to risk. City workers are therefore generally expected to have at least a basic awareness and understanding of the most topical issues affecting their clients' businesses and industries.

Why is commercial awareness important for applicants?

Commercial awareness can provide essential context that enables you to better understand commercial case studies and business-related assessment centre questions. It can also help to prepare you for internships and ultimately, a graduate role. For example, commercial awareness can help you to participate in informed discussions with interviewers and supervisors, better prepare for mock presentations and research reports, and better understand the context of the work you are set. Being "commercially aware" can therefore help to demonstrate your interest in and enthusiasm towards the firm's clients and the work it carries out.

How can commercial awareness come up in interviews?

These days, graduate employers tend to look for commercial "interest" as much as (if not more than) commercial "awareness". You won't be expected to detail every single commercial, political and economic event that has happened over the past few years, but you may be expected to demonstrate an interest in business and the broader commercial factors that can affect the firm and its clients. Commercial awareness may be tested in various ways during interviews. You may be asked to define "commercial awareness" and explain its relevance to the firm's employees. You may be asked to speak about a particular news story that has interested you or be asked point blank about a specific event that has recently occurred; however this kind of question is phrased, be ready to put forward an opinion and explain how the story or event could impact the firm and its clients. You may also be presented with a commercial case study or fictitious client/business scenario, which could require you to demonstrate your understanding of various business, financial and (depending on the context) legal concepts.

How can you demonstrate commercial awareness?

You may well have demonstrated commercial awareness even if you haven't previously worked for a business. If asked to discuss a time when you have demonstrated commercial awareness, you could try to draw analogies between the fundamental processes that businesses follow, and some of the roles you have taken during your previous experiences. These processes might include creating a product (or defining a service), branding and marketing your offering, budgeting, setting prices that allow for a profit, dealing with customers, recruiting and managing others, and a broad range of other considerations.

For example, if you have arranged a university ball, then you will likely have been involved in: creating a product (the ball); branding that product (deciding which theme to go with and how to reflect this theme in the decorations and entertainment); setting the ticket price and budgeting (you will need to ensure that ticket sales and sponsorship will at least cover the cost of hiring a venue, catering, entertainment and decorations); marketing (trying to persuade people to buy tickets); customer service (responding to questions from prospective attendees); recruitment (recruiting junior executive committee members to help out); managing others (making sure team members are fulfilling their roles on time); and a range of other commercial activities.

Current affairs and industry trends

What questions might you be asked?

Firms may want to see evidence of your interest in and understanding of current affairs and the industry you are looking to work in. In this context, you might be asked to discuss a recent commercial news story or comment more generally on the industry trends that affect the firm and its clients.

Q. What have you read about in the news recently?

Q. How does [*particular news article*] relate to the firm and its clients?

Q. What are the major challenges facing the firm / industry?

Q. What is your opinion on [*topical news story*]?

Q. If you could make one change to the law, what would it be?

Q. Over the next 12 to 18 months, which industry developments do you feel will have the greatest impact on the firm?

Q. If you received £1 million, how would you invest it?

News stories

In the majority of my interviews, I was – at least to some extent – able to lead the direction of the interview when discussing current affairs. Rather than facing unexpected questions about random events, I was usually asked to talk about something that I had recently read in the news or something relating to another statement I had made. For example, if you mention one of the firm's previous deals or discuss a current topical story in your application, this may well come up during your interview. However, if there is a particular topic that is consistently discussed on the front pages prior to your interview (for instance, regulation, tax avoidance, a pandemic, political instability, elections, disasters, emerging markets etc.), then try to gain some insight into the topic before the interview, just in case the interviewer brings it up.

Also be sure to check the front page of the Financial Times on the morning of your interview, just in case something major has happened. I would have been caught out had I not checked the Financial Times on the morning of my very first interview, as a major change had been announced relating to the main topic that I had prepared to discuss in the interview. The interviewer of course brought up this change as soon as discussions relating to that topic began, and had I not known what the interviewer was talking about, who knows whether I would have been offered an internship (as it may well have come across as though I had only a superficial interest in current affairs).

Once you have read around a particular topic, it's important that you consider the potential impact of that topic on the firm and/or its clients. For example, if you are discussing newly implemented regulation that restricts companies' ability to minimise their tax liabilities or investors' ability to lend or invest, consider whether this could impede the ability of those affected by the regulation to maintain or exceed their levels of profitability.

- If banks are more restricted in their ability to lend or corporations face higher tax bills, could this indicate their profit levels will reduce? Could this in turn indicate that they may be unable to continuing investing or expanding to the same extent in the future? If so, how might this affect the firm? Could it result in a reduction in the amount of M&A work available in the market?

- Conversely, could new regulation provide any opportunities for the firm? For instance, might clients require assistance to help them understand and comply with the new regulation?

If there is an oil crisis and some of the firms' major clients are oil companies, how will this affect those clients' financial performances? Could lower profits mean those clients invest in fewer transactions, thus reducing their need for legal advice? How might the firm be able to support those clients? Could those clients need help managing disputes relating to the oil crisis? In addition, could the firm hedge its position by pursuing other opportunities or industries?

If you are discussing a weakened economy or an influx of corporate insolvencies, could the economic climate provide any opportunities for the firm's insolvency practice (if it has one)? Moreover, could there be a general increase in disputes as companies sue each other to recover payments owed in the fear that their debtors will otherwise become insolvent and thus default on the debt? Is the firm's litigation practice well placed to win this type of work? Conversely, might companies be more hesitant to engage in M&A and if so, how could this affect the firm's deal flow?

Industry trends and challenges

Many prospective employers also ask about the industry trends and challenges that they are navigating, so try to research these and form opinions on how whatever you are reading might affect your prospective employer, its clients and the markets in which those clients operate. For example, if you read that clients are increasingly looking for greater value for money, whilst the industry has become heavily saturated (meaning firms may have to increasingly compete on price), think about how this could affect firms from a business perspective. Is it becoming harder to compete? If so, how could the firm respond? Should the firm expand into less saturated markets? Should it consider opening a new office in one of these markets and if so, where? Alternatively, should the firm develop innovative ways to provide additional value to clients? Either way, try to consider what actions the firm could take to capitalise on any opportunities or mitigate any threats. Remember, different firms will experience different challenges depending on their size, sector-focus and specialisms, so do not prepare generic answers to use across the board.

Structuring discussions about current affairs and industry trends

When presenting on or discussing a particular topic, you should start by giving a broad overview of the topic, just to give context. Next, you could give some specific examples from the news, for instance by mentioning some of the companies affected or involved in the story. This will help to show that you have read around (and taken an interest in) the topic. If possible, you should then attempt some critical analysis, perhaps by outlining any applicable pros and cons, differing opinions and/or potential implications for stakeholders (e.g. suppliers or consumers) and the relevant industry. You should also perhaps explain why you found the story interesting, and be prepared to give your own opinion on any of the points you have raised (or any other points that the interviewers might pick up on). You could then conclude, if appropriate, by explaining how the story relates to the firm and its clients (e.g. could there be opportunities to win more work, a possible reduction in certain workstreams, opportunities to advise on compliance with new laws, and so on.

Broad overview of the topic → Specific examples from the news → Critical analysis → Tie the story into the firm and its clients

Commercial case studies

As part of a commercial assessment, you may also have to complete commercial case studies, evaluate fictitious client/business scenarios or tackle interviews that require you to discuss, for example, key business concepts, commercial risks and opportunities, different options for financing deals, mergers and acquisitions and more. You may also have to explain the role of the firm/different departments when advising clients in different contexts.

These types of assessments may require you to complete a written report, deliver a brief presentation on information that you have been provided and/or answer a number of questions on business issues and how a firm can assist its clients. As part of this process, you may need to identify certain risks and suggest how these could be mitigated; draw out potential opportunities and suggest strategies that could be employed to capitalise on each; recommend which steps a fictitious client should take; or compare various options (e.g. potential acquisition or investment targets), then form an opinion on which to pursue and justify this decision. For example if a client is considering purchasing another firm, what are the different financing options available and the corresponding advantages and disadvantages of each? How could such a transaction be structured? What are the primary risks and how can they be mitigated? How can the firm help? These types of questions are covered in the City Career Series Commercial Law, Investment Banking and Consultancy Handbooks, mentioned again below.

Frameworks such as those below can act as checklists to help you identify any points or angles that you might not have already considered, and ensure that you're covering all relevant bases. They can also help you to process and organise the information you receive during a commercial awareness or case study interview, which in turn can enable you to structure presentations and discussions in a way that your interviewers can easily follow (i.e. coherently, without overlapping points). To that end, I used the SWOT framework when processing information in the context of an interview case study, as it helped me to quickly structure my thoughts under pressure when preparing to deliver a presentation on a large volume of content.

However, it's important that you carefully consider the precise questions you're asked, and that you don't stick too rigidly to a particular framework structure if this would involve departing from your brief or failing to structure answers in a way that makes sense in the context. In such cases, use them only for inspiration and support.

SWOT analysis

A SWOT analysis can be used to conduct an internal review of how a business is performing and how well it is positioned to take advantage of present/future opportunities and tackle any present/future challenges. It involves assessing the **S**trengths and **W**eaknesses of a business (internal factors), alongside the **O**pportunities from which it could potentially benefit and **T**hreats that it could face (external factors relating to the market/industry in which the business operates).

Strengths

Which positive attributes does the company possess? Does it have unique resources that contribute towards its success? Examples include: unique/popular products, unrivalled research capabilities, particularly talented employees, strong customer loyalty and strong branding. Does the company have a competitive advantage?

Weaknesses

Which negative attributes does the company exhibit? Is it struggling financially? Are its products outdated? Does it lack strong brand recognition? Has the company tried to deal with its weaknesses?

Opportunities

Which opportunities are currently available for the company to exploit? Is its market growing? Is consumer behaviour changing in a way that could benefit the company? Are other opportunities likely to arise in the future?

Threats

Which external factors could negatively impact upon the company? Is its market shrinking? Is the market becoming saturated? Is the government regulating the market more heavily? Are consumers spending less (e.g. is there a recession)? Are these factors affecting all firms in the industry, or the company in particular?

PESTLE analysis

A PESTLE analysis can help you to outline the impact that political (**P**), economic (**E**), socio-cultural (**S**) technological (**T**), legal (**L**) and environmental (**E**) factors have on a particular industry (and thus the businesses operating within that industry).

Political
Consider the influence/impact government policies may have on the overall economy and/or a particular industry, including tax, fiscal and trade policies. Consider whether political instability, relations between jurisdictions, pressure groups, corruption or bureaucracy could impact upon an industry's profitability.

Economic
Consider how the local/global economy is performing and how this could impact upon firms in a particular industry. Are consumers generally spending money or saving? How do inflation rates, tax rates, interest rates and exchange rates impact upon industry profitability levels? Is the industry growing? Is there ample foreign direct investment occurring? Do these factors affect the way businesses price their products/services?

Social
Consider the social factors (including cultural aspects and consumer attitudes) that affect consumer demand and the way businesses operate. For instance, what are the typical purchasing patterns/cultural trends that consumers tend to follow? Do consumers make purchases that correlate with seasons/holidays? What are the key demographics and how easily can these be targeted? Are there ethical issues that affect the media/consumers' perception of the industry (and firms operating within that industry)?

Technological
Consider the technological innovations on which the industry currently relies/may rely upon in the future. Do these impact favourably upon the industry? Will businesses within that industry need to constantly innovate in order to compete? How important is intellectual property? Examples of technology include automation (automated manufacturing, distribution etc.), information and communications (for instance, traders in an investment bank rely heavily on technology to ensure they can execute trades effectively) and research and development.

Legal
Consider the legislation that affects businesses within the industry. How stringent is consumer law, employment law, health and safety law, competition law etc. in a particular jurisdiction? Does relevant industry-specific legislation exist? What impact does international legislation have on the ability of businesses within that industry to sell to customers in other jurisdictions? How is the legal landscape likely to change?

Environmental
Consider how environmental factors may impact upon an industry. Could rules relating to waste disposal, climate change or subsidies (e.g. to encourage businesses to adopt strong environmental policies) affect the ability of firms within an industry to generate a profit? How dependent is a particular industry on the weather (consider wind farms, food producers etc.)?

How to build commercial awareness

Trying to "cram" commercial awareness right before an interview isn't an ideal approach, as you'll likely only pick up a shallow understanding of the commercial topics that you read about. If your understanding is shallow, you'll also likely have little interest in what you're reading about and discussing, which won't come across well during an interview. Think about the first few pages of a dense novel. It's harder to maintain your interest at the start, as you don't yet understand the context or the history of the characters. It's the history and the developments that draw you in, meaning stories tend to become far more gripping once you start to understand how the sections you are reading fit into the broader context of the book. It's the same with commercial awareness. News stories and commercial concepts are not generally interesting in isolation, but once you start to understand how the pieces fit together – and the impact this can all have on firms, clients and industries – you'll likely find it all a lot more interesting and become more confident talking about it in interviews.

It's better to get into the habit of building your commercial awareness on a regular basis, and even 5 minutes per day can make all the difference. You'll be surprised at how much more interested you become in business news and commercial concepts more generally once you have started to understand the bigger picture. To that end, I'm now going to cover a collection of recommended resources that you can use to help build your commercial awareness. In addition, get in the habit of looking up definitions for any terms you don't understand (the Investopedia website provides really great explanations of thousands of key business terms, commercial concepts and City jargon) and information about companies mentioned in the news that you don't recognise. And do whatever's necessary to help you retain the information you pick up. Discuss news stories with others, write notes in your own words, record yourself presenting on topics...whatever works.

To learn more about commercial awareness and how to build it, and to enhance your commercial, financial and legal knowledge (including your understanding of the terminology, jargon and acronyms used in practice), check out:

www.commerciallaw.academy/courses/commercial-awareness
www.commerciallaw.academy/courses/mergers-acquisitions
www.commerciallaw.academy/courses/interview-case-studies
www.commerciallaw.academy/courses/launching-a-business

Business news

You should get into the habit of reading the news daily, if only for a few minutes. You will soon build a comprehensive knowledge and understanding of what is going on in the business areas relevant to the organisations to which you are applying. There are many sources you can use to build your awareness, knowledge and understanding of current affairs. BBC Business News (online) is probably my favourite source for readings about the news, as the articles are short, concise and (generally) jargon-free. Helpfully, these articles also tend to include a series of "related" links at the bottom, which can help you to trace back the history of a particular event or trend, and access supplementary information (such as the range of opinions around a particular story). Reading these related articles can help you to build a more comprehensive understanding of different topics.

I used to copy and paste major headlines from news websites into a Word document, the add to the document as related stories and developments emerged. This helped to boost my general knowledge and understanding of what was going on in the world, whilst also providing a consolidated document that I could quickly and conveniently refer back to before interviews to remind myself of the news stories that I have followed. You might also want to place an additional focus on two to three topical issues that really engage and interest you. Research them in greater depth and consider not only the debate and critical analysis surrounding the issues, but also the ways in which the issues could affect City firms and their clients. I created mini reports, which really helped me to prepare for in-depth discussions about the stories during interviews.

Commercial news digests

Signing up to news digests can help to get you in the habit of regularly consuming the news in bite-sized chunks. Most digests take only a few minutes to read, but over time they can help you to build a comprehensive picture of what's going on in the world without feeling like you're committing hours and hours to developing your commercial awareness. The Financial Times and The Economist provide solid insights into some of the most relevant topical issues affecting the business, finance and political worlds (and I strongly recommend subscribing to The Economist's free weekly digest email, as this succinctly summarises 8 – 12 of the most important political, economic and commercial news stories). If you're interested in tech, industry trends and the investment landscape, I would also strongly recommend the free weekly digests available from CB Insights and AngelList, and I'm sure there are also countless other digests covering the full spectrum of business-related news.

Online courses

Our **Discussing current affairs and industry trends** course offers in-depth advice from an ex-stock broker on how to research into and confidently discuss current affairs, including how to select which news stories to focus on, what to consider when reading the news, and how to structure your discussions in interviews. The course also includes recordings of our monthly current affairs wrap ups, which offer insights into topical stories from a business, markets and legal perspective). Note that our **Legal technology** course also covers all things legal tech.

www.commerciallaw.academy/courses/current-affairs
www.commerciallaw.academy/courses/legal-technology

Discussing current affairs and industry trends

42 lessons

18.5 hours of video content

Business books

You should aim to develop your business, finance and (where relevant) legal knowledge so that you can demonstrate and apply strong commercial logic during case studies and commercial awareness interviews. Do not just regurgitate definitions. Demonstrate an ability to flexibly apply the concepts to the facts of the case study provided and assess in context which concepts are likely to be the most relevant and effective. There are so many books available to help you build your knowledge of commercial, financial and legal concepts. I personally used Christopher Stoakes' book "All You Need To Know About The City" when preparing for my interviews and I can't recommend it enough (more on this towards the end of this handbook). City Career Series has also published detailed guides designed to provide you with a solid grounding in the key technical concepts that tend to come up in commercial law, investment banking and consulting commercial awareness interviews.

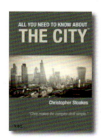     

One of my favourite ways of learning about how businesses operate is by reading books about the history of well-known businesses and founder biographies. I particularly enjoyed "The Upstarts" by Brad Stone, which charts the entrepreneurial journeys of Uber and Air BnB, from the early days of knocking on doors and absorbing rejection after rejection, right through to them joining the realm of tech superstars. I would also recommend Brad Stone's "The Everything Store" (which covers the founding and growth of Amazon) and "Shoe Dog" by the founder of Nike, among others. If there is anything in these books that you don't understand, the Investopedia online dictionary provides really great explanations of thousands of key business terms, commercial concepts and City jargon. Check out www.citycareerseries.com/recommended-resources.php for more recommendations.

Firm news

Even if you are not currently applying to a particular firm, researching the firm in advance and keeping up to date with its deals and announcements could hold you in good stead if you are later required to discuss your motivation for wanting to work at the firm in depth. Read the firm's annual review, news stories on its website, "client alerts" (which tend to summarise relevant political, legal and regulatory developments) and general news articles that mention the firm (Google can be a good place to start). Also consider subscribing to firm newsletters, some of which might give you access to free email digests that can help to keep you abreast of insightful firm, industry and global news. You might also want to follow prospective employers' social media channels, as employers have been known to check to see if you have followed or liked them! On a related note, if you plan to discuss a deal on your application form or during an interview, make sure you carry out sufficient research. For example, you might want to consider: which of the firm's teams contributed, which jurisdictions were involved, what the commercial drivers were, how it was financed, what it means for the relevant stakeholders (customers, suppliers, employees, regulators, competitors etc.), and so on.

Events, webinars, podcasts and other sources

Attending our events and webinars (see https://citycareerseries.clickmeeting.com) – as well as those hosted by City firms, student-focused organisations (e.g. SEO London, Bright Network, Rare Recruitment, LawCareers.Net etc.), university societies, career services, and so on – can also provide a range of opportunities to develop your understanding of current affairs and commercial concepts. If a particular issue has attracted widespread debate (for instance, whether the UK should have left the EU), look for supplementary articles or journals that explore the wider issues surrounding the story. Interviewers may want to see whether you can provide a balanced, critical opinion on the topic (including acknowledgement of the pros and cons where relevant), and these sources can really help. You can also follow well-known commentators and publications on Twitter, subscribe to business podcasts (I highly recommend Watson's Daily's podcast!), join interest groups on platforms such as LinkedIn, delve into blogs focusing on financial services, and watch YouTube videos that focus on topical issues. The list is (almost literally) endless.

Psychometric Tests

Psychometric tests, situational judgment tests and e-tray exercises are used by firms to test certain skills, abilities and thought processes that can indicate a candidate's suitability to a particular role. These tests are also typically used by firms to whittle down vast numbers of applicants to a more manageable pool of interviewees. When assessing the results of these tests, many firms simply require candidates to meet a certain fixed benchmark in order to progress through the relevant stage of the assessment process, although most firms won't reveal what that benchmark is. Although candidates are usually required to complete these tests online from a place of their choosing, some firms may also require candidates to complete tests in person during assessment centres (and these tests may not be computerised). For one firm, I had to complete an online Watson Glaser test during the application stage, then a written version – double the length of the online test – in person, on the day of my interview.

I want to acknowledge at the outset that different approaches to preparing for and tackling tests will better suit different people. There's no single approach that will work for everyone. This is especially the case because psychometric tests usually require some level of natural intuition, although practice can certainly help. With that in mind, I have aimed to provide at least some insight into what these tests can involve, and suggest some tips and techniques that I personally found to be helpful when completing dozens of tests throughout my time at university.

Types of tests

The tests most commonly used by City firms include:

- **Verbal reasoning tests:** these test your understanding of language, including your ability to critically analyse statements, and comprehend, evaluate and apply logic to often complex passages of text.

- **Watson Glaser tests:** these assess your ability to think critically.

- **Logical reasoning tests:** these assess your ability to break down/isolate information and identify patterns or sequences.

- **Numerical reasoning tests:** these assess your ability to quickly and accurately identify, process and analyse numerical data, including statistics.

- **Situational judgement tests**: these assess how you are likely to handle or respond to a variety of scenarios or circumstances that you might encounter if you were to secure an internship or graduate role.

- **Email simulation (or in-tray/e-tray) exercises:** these usually test your ability to identify relevant information, then interpret, process and analyse that information in order to respond to questions under pressure.

Most tests are in a multiple choice format and require you to select only one answer, although the format can of course differ depending on the test provider (and whether firms have commissioned tests that are specifically tailored to their needs). Some tests may also involve negative marking, which means incorrect answers will result in point deductions (as opposed to you simply receiving 0). When this is the case, be particularly careful about blindly guessing answers.

General tips

Pace yourself: all these tests put you under time pressure, so you must strictly pace yourself. Find out how long you have to complete the test and how many questions you will face, then roughly work out the average amount of time that you'll have to answer each question. Don't forget to then monitor the clock throughout!

Avoid getting stuck: it's worth identifying in advance whether you can scroll back between your answers during the test – and change them if necessary – or whether clicking "submit" after selecting an answer means that the answer can no longer be amended (this differs between different types of tests). Either way, don't make the mistake of lingering for too long on one particular question, as you may then run out of time and miss out on the opportunity to answer easier questions later on. You rarely (if ever) need to get 100% of the answers right, so sacrificing one or two tricky questions in the interests of answering *all* the questions you're more comfortable with can be a more efficient and effective use of the allocated time. With tests that let you scroll backwards and forwards between questions, consider noting down the number of each question that you're unable to answer easily, then move swiftly onto to the next. If you have time at the end, you can then go back to the questions that require more thought, safe in the knowledge that you've answered all the others.

Don't look for answer patterns: don't fall into the mindset that, because one answer has come up a few times in a row, the next answer must surely be something else. For all you know, you may have answered one of the previous questions incorrectly!

Verbal reasoning tests

As mentioned, verbal reasoning tests assess your understanding of language, including your ability to critically analyse statements, and comprehend, evaluate and apply logic to often complex passages of text. Employers use a wide variety of tests, although firms often use tests provided by SHL (which tend to include 30 multiple-choice questions that you have 19 minutes to answer).

Verbal reasoning tests typically present you with a primary passage of text, followed by a series of short follow-on statements relating to that text. You then usually need to state whether – based solely on the information contained within the primary passage of text – each of the follow-on statements is true, false, or you cannot say. Select TRUE if the statement is objectively true based only on the information or opinions contained in the passage. Select FALSE if the statement is objectively untrue based only on the information or opinions contained in the passage. And select CANNOT SAY if you cannot objectively determine whether the statement is true or false based on the information given in the primary passage.

Strategies for acing verbal reasoning tests

Carefully read the primary passage before considering the follow-on questions: I find it useful to begin by slowly and carefully reading the whole passage, then subsequently tackling each related statement. Firstly, having read the whole passage, you will know which part to skip to in order to answer each statement. Whilst this means you might not have answered the first question until a couple of minutes have passed, you should be able to answer the other questions relating to the same passage more quickly. Secondly, some passages may start with a snippet that suggests the answer to a particular question or statement is "true", only to then later include a conflicting snippet that indicates the actual answer is "false" or "cannot say". Essentially, if you read the questions first, then skim the passage and stop once you think you have found the answer, you could easily make a mistake. Thirdly, reading the passage *slowly and carefully* can help you to avoid overlooking double negatives or misreading confusing phrases, which are easy mistakes to make when quickly skim reading a passage.

Remember to totally disregard your own general knowledge and opinions: verbal reasoning tests generally require you to *ignore* any external knowledge you may have. Under such circumstances, you are being tested solely on your ability to interpret text, not on your general knowledge, so the questions must be answered based solely on the information contained in the primary passages of text. To help remember this, you could try tacking on the phrase "According to the passage…" to each of the short follow-on statements before deciding which answer to pick.

Don't get caught out by generalisations: sometimes a primary passage of text might state that "some" people think or do something, whereas one of the follow-on statements might claim that "all" people think or do that thing. In such circumstances, the correct answer would likely be "Cannot Say", because you can't conclude that "all" people do something if the passage only confirms that "some" do. In other words, don't make generalisations based on statements made about select groups of people. For example, if the primary passage discusses how some lawyers quit their jobs because they are unhappy, and the follow-on statement proposes that "all lawyers quit their jobs because they are unhappy", the answer would be "Cannot Say" (or "False", if there is something in the primary passage that confirms at least one lawyer has quit their job for an alternative reason). You should therefore always consider whether words such as "few", "some", "all", "many", "most", "none", "sometimes", "always" and "never" are used, as these words can indicate whether you are able to draw conclusions based on generalisations.

Don't make assumptions: don't make assumptions based on your own logic; remember to focus only on what you are explicitly told in the main passage. For example, if the primary passage states that a certain proportion of lawyers quit their jobs because they are unhappy, and the follow-on statement claims that the lawyers who quit their jobs were unhappy because of long working hours, the correct answer would be "Cannot Say". Whilst in reality the lawyers' unhappiness may well derive from working long hours, you cannot conclude that the statement is true, because the primary passage of text doesn't explicitly confirm this. There may have been other reasons behind their unhappiness, for example the nature of the work they were receiving, a lack of intellectual fulfilment, or the culture of their teams. Sometimes, trying to think of alternative circumstances or scenarios in this way can help you to determine whether a follow-on statement is making a generalisation that isn't supported by the main passage of text. Remember however that if the main passage of text tells you that lawyers are only ever unhappy because of long working hours, then you would need to disregard any other plausible scenarios and take it as objectively true that lawyers are only ever unhappy because of long working hours.

Don't assume a cause-and-effect relationship: don't assume that a cause-and-effect relationship exists between two separate statements made in a primary passage of text. Such statements may not be directly related, unless you are explicitly told otherwise. For example, a primary passage may state that some lawyers are unhappy and separately state that some lawyers quit their jobs, without actually connecting these two statements (e.g. by explicitly stating that unhappiness is the reason behind the resignations). In such circumstances, if the follow-on statement proclaims that "some lawyers quit their jobs because they are unhappy", the answer would be "Cannot Say", even though your own logic might dictate that the statement in reality is probably true. This is why candidates often incorrectly select "True" over "Cannot Say" in such circumstances.

Create a flow chart: consider sketching out flow charts to help you identify, break down and understand the logic presented within each primary passage of text. However, only take this approach if you're able to work quickly, as you'll be under time pressure.

Watson Glaser tests

The Watson Glaser test is often the first hurdle that must be surmounted during the recruitment process for large City law firms. Unlike common aptitude tests that assess a range of skills and competencies, the Watson Glaser test focuses only on critical thinking. Note that the Watson Glaser test is not as time pressured as many other critical thinking tests: with an average of 45 seconds to answer each question, most candidates are able to complete the tests on time.

However, psychometric testing experts consider it to be one of the trickiest tests out there for two key reasons. Firstly, it is an objectively difficult test, with its own sets of rules and a unique question format. Secondly, applicant scores are benchmarked against the scores of other applicants. This means that there doesn't tend to be a set "pass" rate. Applicants with the highest scores relative to other applicants will progress through to the next stage of the application process, meaning you have to beat the scores of a certain number of other applicants to progress.

The key sections

The tests are split into five distinct sections – inferences, assumptions, deduction, interpretation and arguments – and the rules change between each of these sections. As with verbal reasoning tests, you're typically presented with a primary passage of text, followed by a series of short follow-on statements relating to that text. However, the nature of the passages and follow-on statements, and the range of answers you're required to give, differ between sections.

Inferences: in this section, you'll be presented with a primary passage of text, followed by a series of inferences (i.e. a series of statements containing proposed conclusions that are potentially based on the primary passage of text). You must then decide whether each corresponding inference is true, probably true, false, probably false, or whether there simply isn't enough information within the passage for you to draw one of these conclusions. Inferences are particularly tricky, as you need to consider the degree of truth or falsity when determining whether a particular inference is "Probably true" or "Probably false", and at times this may require you to draw upon common knowledge (i.e. information that practically everyone knows). However, remember not to do so when determining whether an inference is "True" or "False", as these answers must be fully supported by the statements in the primary passage.

Assumptions: in this section, you'll be presented with a primary statement, followed by a series of proposed assumptions. You must then decide whether the maker of the primary statement must have based their statement or conclusion on the assumptions presented. You should then select "Assumption made" if you think that a proposed assumption is taken for granted in the primary statement, or "Assumption not made" if you think a proposed assumption is not necessarily taken for granted.

Deduction: in this section, you'll be presented with a primary passage of text, followed by a series of proposed conclusions. You must then determine whether each of these proposed conclusions can be reached based *only* on the information presented in the primary passage of text. You should then select "Conclusion follows" if you think the conclusion can be reached based *only* on the information presented in the primary passage of text, or "Conclusion does not follow" if you don't. Even if you know that a certain proposed conclusion is true (or likely to be true), if you cannot confirm this based only on the information presented within the primary passage, then you cannot resolve that the conclusion follows.

Interpretation: in this section, you'll be presented with a primary passage of text, followed by a series of proposed conclusions. You must then determine whether each of the proposed conclusions logically flows – beyond reasonable doubt – from the information presented in the primary passage of text. You should then select "Conclusion follows" if you think the conclusion follows *beyond reasonable doubt* based (only) on the information presented in the primary passage of text, even though the conclusion may not follow absolutely. Or select "Conclusion does not follow" if you don't.

Arguments: in this section, you'll be presented with a series of questions, each of which will be followed by a "yes" or "no" answer, as well as a proposed argument to support that "yes" or "no" answer. You must then determine whether that proposed argument is "Weak" or "Strong" (i.e. you must assess whether the argument provides strong support for the "yes" or "no" answer given). For an argument to be strong, it must be *important* (i.e. it must address the key issue being discussed/go to the heart of the question) and it must *directly relate* to the question. An argument is weak if it does not *directly* relate to the question, if it is of only *minor* importance, or if it is directly related to only *trivial* aspects of the question. Note that an argument can still be strong even if that argument alone wouldn't necessarily be enough to conclusively determine the answer to the question, or if other (arguably even stronger) arguments exist in favour of or against whatever is being proposed.

Strategies for acing Watson Glaser tests

Carefully read the primary passage before considering the follow-on questions: as with verbal reasoning tests, I find it useful to begin by slowly and carefully reading the whole passage before tackling each related statement.

Know the rules: the Watson Glaser test has its own sets of rules, unparalleled by those of other critical thinking tests. This means you need to shift your mindset as you progress between sections, which requires a strong level of understanding and intellectual discipline. For this reason, it is critical to familiarise yourself with the rules, ideally through practising using material that has been specifically designed to replicate the types of questions you will face (more on this below).

Learn to ignore irrelevant information: whilst completing these tests, you'll often need to ignore your intuition and predispositions. Other than in the inferences section (in accordance with the explanation above), you must totally disregard your own general knowledge, biases and opinions so that you're basing your answers solely on the information contained in the primary passages of text. To that end, to reach the correct answers, you must sometimes go against what you believe to be true in the most fundamental way.

Don't linger on tricky questions for too long: unlike some psychometric tests, Watson Glaser tests usually let you scroll back and forth between your answers – and change them if necessary – before you submit your test. For this reason (as mentioned earlier), it can be better to initially defer questions that you can't easily answer, just to make sure that you get through the whole test and answer all the questions that you are comfortable answering.

For an in-depth look at Watson Glaser tests, including practice test questions from all five sections and practical tips on how to improve your technique, check out: **www.commerciallaw.academy/courses/psychometric-tests**

Logical reasoning tests

Logical reasoning tests (also known as "abstract reasoning" tests) are designed to assess your ability to quickly identify patterns, sequences, rules and trends. This can give employers an insight into your ability to break down and analyse problems and think strategically about potential solutions. Many City firms use logical reasoning tests produced by SHL. These typically present you with a horizontal sequence of images, followed by a series of options for what the next image in the sequence should look like. Each image in the main sequence will change slightly in accordance with a particular pattern or set of rules and you'll need to identify this pattern or set of rules in order to ascertain what you would expect the final image in the chain to look like.

Strategies for acing logical reasoning tests

Within each image that forms part of the main sequence, there will usually be a number of different elements, for example shapes, lines and/or images. You should start by breaking down the first image in the sequence into its constituent parts. Once you have isolated each element within the first image (e.g. each shape or line), then – one by one – you should track how each element moves, changes or evolves as it progresses through the sequence of images. This should help you to identify whether each element follows a particular pattern, which will enable you to infer how each element should appear in the final image of the sequence.

Practising these tests can help you to get in the habit of quickly zoning out different elements and assessing which patterns might apply. However, there may be elements in each image that act as decoys, meaning they don't follow a particular pattern, so don't spend a disproportionate amount of time focusing on any one element. In such cases, as long as you can identify patterns that are followed by one or two elements, you should be able to identify the correct answer from the options presented.

Patterns to look out for

The patterns in logical reasoning tests tend to vary and some are more complicated than others – I still come across some that I have no idea how to solve! – but here are examples of some of the patterns that you should look out for when analysing sequences.

☒ **Colour:** you may, for instance, be presented with some black shapes and some white shapes. Check whether the shapes change colour as you progress through the sequence (e.g. every image or every other image).

☒ **Rotation, position and/or direction:** you may have lines or shapes that rotate or move around the image. If so, check how often they move/rotate. Are they moving in a particular direction (e.g. clockwise) along a line or around a series of squares? Are their movements triggered by something within the image (for example, an arrow that changes colour or moves)? Do the movements occur consistently as you progress through the sequence of images (for example, does every new image host the line or shape in a different position)?

☒ **Quantity:** you may have elements – for instance shapes or lines – that change in quantity throughout the sequence. Is there a pattern you can pick up on that dictates when an extra line or shape will appear or disappear? For example, the 1st image might contain 1 circle, the 2nd image might contain 2 circles, the 3rd image might contain 3 circles, and so on.

☒ **Size:** If there are shapes contained within another shape (for example, a circle containing a smaller triangle, which in turn contains an even smaller square), try to see whether one of the shapes from the 1st image reappears in the 2nd image in some form. Does the largest shape in the 1st image – i.e. the circle – become the smallest shape in the 2nd image? Does the shape in the middle of the 1st image – i.e. the triangle – become the largest shape in the 2nd image? It's worth checking.

Whatever you do, don't panic. When a new set of images flashes up on the screen, they may make little sense for the first few seconds. When this happens, keep calm and break down each image methodically in order to work towards discovering the answer. If there are all sorts of shapes in each image, and the sequence doesn't appear to follow any particular pattern, then try looking only at the colour or number of shapes (or if there is a diagonal line in the middle, then the number of shapes on either side of the line). The pattern may well be simpler than you initially suspect.

Numerical reasoning tests

Numerical reasoning tests are designed to assess your ability to quickly and accurately identify, process and analyse numerical data, including statistics. Most numerical reasoning questions require only basic arithmetic, with the required calculations usually focusing on addition, subtraction, multiplication, division and calculating percentages or fractions. This means you don't need to be a maths genius to determine the right answers. Personally, I had not studied Maths for around 7 years (and was not particularly confident with numbers) when I first faced these tests. However, I still managed to pass them, even though friends of mine studying numbers-focused degrees failed on a number of occasions. Note that I have never seen a law firm set a standalone numerical reasoning test as part of its recruitment process, although I have completed an email simulation exercise which included a few questions that were similar to numerical reasoning test questions.

Numerical reasoning tests typically present you with a graph or table containing numbers and percentages, then ask a series of questions that require you to identify specific numbers from the graph or table and then plug those numbers into one or more calculations to reach the correct answer. These tables or graphs may contain data relating to a broad range of subjects, for example, different companies, locations, product lines, sales figures or periods of time.

Strategies for acing numerical reasoning tests

Whilst the types of calculations expected of you may be fairly simple, numerical reasoning tests tend to put you under extreme time pressure, especially if certain questions require you to carry out multiple calculations in order to determine the answers. An ability to work quickly, calmly and accurately is therefore crucial.

Attention to detail is also essential, as if you don't accurately identify the correct figures to plug into your calculations, then you won't reach the right answers. No matter how good you are at maths. If you're faced with a table of data, make sure you carefully read the headings along the top and down the side before selecting which numbers to focus on. And with graphs, pay attention to the axes, the key, and any additional information contained within the graph itself. Also, have a calculator, some paper and a pen ready. Then perhaps start by reading each question very carefully and then isolating and noting down the relevant figures from the table or graph before making any calculations. Taking this approach can help you to avoid accidentally including the wrong information in your calculations as a result of focusing on too much at once.

Situational judgement tests

Situational judgment tests are psychological tools used to evaluate candidates' behavioural traits, social intelligence and cognitive abilities, with a view to measuring each candidate's suitability to the employer and the role for which they are applying. These types of tests might assess, for example, a candidate's ability to work in a team, motivate others, prioritise tasks, delegate effectively, support supervisors and senior colleagues, interact with clients, problem solve, and think laterally, whilst offering an insight into their thought processes (including their judgment and approach to decision-making). Note that these tests are increasingly also being used during interviews, with candidates having to discuss scenarios in more detail with their interviewers.

Situational judgment tests are typically designed to give employers insights into how you are likely to handle or respond to certain scenarios or circumstances that you might encounter if you were to secure an internship or graduate role at the firm. As firms tend to have different cultures and expectations, situational judgment tests are often tailored to each employer's specific requirements. This means that, unlike with certain other types of psychometric tests, you're less likely to face the same scenarios and questions from different employers.

Situational judgment tests typically present you with a hypothetical work-related scenario, followed by, for example: a list of proposed actions that you could take in the given scenario; a list of potential responses to the circumstances presented; and/or a list of potential behaviours that could be adopted in light of the situation. You will then usually be expected to choose what you deem to be the most or least suitable option from the list in light of the scenario (i.e. the option that best correlates with how you would act or respond in the particular circumstances). Alternatively, you may be asked to rank the proposed courses of action, responses or behaviours by their level of appropriateness or effectiveness.

Strategies for acing situational judgment tests

Read all the information you are given before making a decision: there may be a number of potentially sensible or reasonable options for each corresponding scenario, so it's imperative that you read the question carefully and properly assess every option before submitting your answer.

Focus only on the information contained within the question: avoid making any assumptions about the context of the scenarios presented; only consider the information you are explicitly provided when assessing the circumstances and reviewing the proposed responses or courses of action.

Research the employer and the nature of the role in advance: when assessing proposed responses or courses of action, always bear in mind what the firm is likely to expect from its employees in terms of (for example) attitude, commitment, working hours and flexibility. Also consider the nature of the role for which you are applying, as this can determine what's expected of you. For example, if you are applying for a high pressure client-facing role that you know involves long hours at times, then remember this if questioned on how you would react if you were asked to cancel your social plans at a moment's notice in order to work on an urgent task that has unexpectedly come in at the last minute. The nature of the role might suggest that the employer expects you to select whichever response involves working longer hours and being flexible with your time. Similarly, if you are applying for a role for which accuracy and attention to detail are very important, then bear this in mind if a question is asking whether you would rush through a piece of work in a particular context.

In addition, don't forget that firms might differ in terms of the types of responses they expect, meaning there is no such thing as an "objectively correct" answer for every scenario. Context is key. This is why it's important to take into account the types of behaviours that each prospective employer will likely be looking for.

Be honest: it's important to remember that these tests are not designed to catch you out. They're designed to test your suitability to the firm and for the role. If you answer questions honestly and do not proceed through that round of the assessment process, then perhaps that firm was not the right firm for you. It may simply be that your priorities and expectations do not align with what the firm expects, so working there might have been a miserable experience for you anyway. On the flip side, if you respond with what you *think* the firm is looking for – rather than answering honestly – you risk being rejected from the process on the basis of answers that didn't genuinely reflect how you would have reacted in reality!

Email simulation exercises

Email simulation exercises (sometimes referred to as "in-tray" or "e-tray" exercises) are usually designed to help firms evaluate your ability to carry out the types of tasks that you could face if you were working in the role, meaning these tests can come in many different forms and are usually tailored to each firm. You will likely be assessed on your ability to identify relevant information, then interpret, process and analyse that information in order to respond to questions under pressure. As part of this, you will need to demonstrate your organisational and time management skills, ability to work under pressure, proficiency using computers, and attention to detail. On that note, be sure to carefully read and follow any instructions you receive!

These exercises are typically based within a programme that looks like an email client, complete with a fictional inbox and folders containing information. Emails typically flow into this "inbox" over a set period of time and contain the types of questions and requests you may receive during a graduate scheme. Note that these tests can come in a variety of forms however, with some firms instead providing you with printed documents or an electronic document containing various emails, questions and exercises.

Fictional emails can cover a whole host of tasks and topics. You may be required to provide an update on a particular matter, or to ascertain the amount owed by a particular client to date. You may be asked to identify to whom a particular email or request should be forwarded. You may need to solve specific problems or recommend commercial courses of action. You may have to decide how best to delegate a particular task or which emails or issues should be prioritised. You might have to proofread something. Some questions might look a little like situational judgment or numerical reasoning questions. And so on.

Email simulation exercises commonly present questions in a multiple-choice format, and you will usually need to base your answers on information provided before or during the test. For example, during one test that I completed, the relevant information was contained within a variety of documents, each of which had been buried within a structure of folders and sub folders. Having to quickly find the relevant information definitely added to the time pressure and meant I had to work accurately and methodically to complete the test on time.

Strategies for acing email simulation exercises

If you're told in advance how many emails you will need to deal with, be sure to keep track of your progress throughout the exercise. Emails may come into the inbox over a period of time and may disappear once you have responded to them, so if you don't note down the number you have dealt with, you may be unable to ascertain how many more you will need to deal with before your time is up. This can make it very difficult to pace yourself, as I learned first-hand when completing my first email simulation exercise.

In addition, if you are given reading time at the start, make sure you at least skim through all the available folders and documents in advance, as at least you will then have a rough idea of where to start looking during the test. When completing one particular test, I spent so much time trying to write notes during the reading time that I only managed to go through half of the folders and documents before the emails started to flow. This meant I had to go through dozens of folders mid-test in order to identify relevant information, which – needless to say – resulted in a pretty stressful experience.

Converting Internships Into Full-time Jobs

Internships give firms the opportunity to assess both your character and your suitability – to the firm and to the role – in much greater depth. Firms will likely evaluate the way you approach your work and the quality of the work you deliver. Firms will assess your interactions with employees and other interns and how well you are able to work in a team. And firms will look at which candidates remain enthusiastic and seem genuinely interested in both the firm and the career.

Demonstrating your motivation and enthusiasm

You are selling yourself during an internship as much as a firm is selling itself to you, so your personality, character and performance will influence a firm's inclination (or not!) to hire you. In particular, your attitude, body language and general behaviour will affect whether a firm believes you have the ability to complete work in a very demanding, client-led environment and whether you can be trusted to work with high-profile clients and professional services firms that expect only the best from advisors and colleagues.

Enthusiasm

Many candidates are rejected following an internship on the basis that the firm felt their enthusiasm was lacking. It is easy to assume that if you are clever enough to do the work required of you, then surely this should be enough. However, if you do not seem enthusiastic and willing to learn when spending only a few weeks (or months) at the firm, this could give the impression that after working there for a year, perhaps you will no longer care at all. Moreover, a firm might be concerned that in the longer-term, a lack of enthusiasm could also affect the quality and consistency of your work, impact negatively upon the teams you work with, and adversely affect the firm's culture more generally. You can demonstrate enthusiasm simply by getting involved in as much as you can, asking insightful questions, and always remaining outwardly positive (after all, it's not difficult to smile for a few weeks!).

Culture

Firms will look to see how well you fit in with the firm's culture, including whether you are able to build a rapport with those around you. They want to recruit people who can get on with *anyone*, so remain open and approachable and try to meet as many people as you can. Perhaps ask a variety of employees if they'll meet you for coffee (this will also provide an opportunity to access further insights into the firm and career). You should also attend as many social and networking events as possible – both optional and mandatory – as doing so can demonstrate your interest in integrating into the firm, getting to know your potential future colleagues (this includes other interns, so don't neglect them!), and contributing to the firm's culture. So make the most of the opportunities on offer. Perhaps even try to get involved in sports teams, music ensembles, diversity initiatives, employee networks, pro bono work and the like. It's absolutely fine if there are any work-related (e.g. tight deadlines) or cultural circumstances that impinge upon your ability to attend certain events, but perhaps explain the situation to the graduate recruitment team in advance. Finally, although it goes without saying, don't get too drunk and don't cross any boundaries! Remember that you're being continually assessed, even if it seems – on the face of it – as if those around you won't mind. You just never know.

Attitude and motivation

Firms will also look for a genuine commitment to your chosen career; they will want to see that you have shown a real interest in the work and the firm more broadly, as they would rather not invest in you if you're likely to leave a short way into your career. In fact, leading City firm Clifford Chance one said in an article they wrote for an earlier edition of this handbook that "although technical skills are important at this stage to some extent, attitude is by far the best indicator of whether an intern is likely to thrive during our training programme. At the end of the day, if you have successfully progressed through the assessment process, we already know you have the capabilities to succeed; the internship is simply our opportunity to see you in action." And if you have interned elsewhere, don't let this affect your attitude (I've seen this before, and it didn't go down well).

Do your research before starting the scheme, so that you can demonstrate knowledge of the firm's departments, experience, clients, industries and so on from the get-go. Then ask lots of carefully considered questions during the scheme – to supervisors, graduate recruiters, people you meet during socials, employees who deliver presentations – as this can demonstrate your genuine interest in the firm (and don't forget to note down the answers!). During the scheme, if you have not received work from your supervisor, then talk to them about it. You could always (with your supervisor's permission) offer other individuals – or even other departments – a helping hand.

When it comes to carrying out the work, keep an open mind and approach all tasks with enthusiasm. Recognise that every task can provide a learning opportunity, including the more menial or administrative tasks. For example, if you're asked to proofread a long, complex document, don't sulk and act as if the work is beneath you. Focus on the fact that you're receiving valuable exposure to an unfamiliar document that you may one day have to draft yourself, and be thankful that the task isn't beyond your capabilities. After all, it's better to have the opportunity to do a solid job on a simple task rather than being thrown in at the deep end and screwing up a far more complex or substantive task. Plus, the next time you come across that document, it will seem more familiar, meaning you'll be better placed to take on a more substantive role (without screwing up!). You could also use the opportunity to ask questions about the context so that you can learn more about – and demonstrate your interest in – the document and how it fits into the bigger picture. This is the mindset that firms will be looking for. It's all part of the learning process.

If you can't do the work to the standard expected, the firm will be unlikely to offer you a job. Whilst some pieces of work will be harder than others – and minor mistakes may be completely understandable – you should always strive to demonstrate strong attention to detail. Proofread your work multiple times (you could even ask colleagues to have a read if you think this is appropriate) and ensure there are no spelling, grammatical or formatting errors. Essentially, avoid any easily avoidable mistakes! And as mentioned, ask questions about the wider context of the work to demonstrate your interest and peripheral understanding.

House style

Check to see whether there are particular fonts, templates or settings in Word or Excel that firms use as part of their "house style", and if there are, adhere to these where possible. Doing so can demonstrate your ability to absorb and adapt to the ways in which the firm operates, whilst also ensuring that the people judging your work will approve of it stylistically. On that note, PowerPoint and handout templates can be especially useful if you're tasked with delivering an assessed pitch or presentation during the scheme. There may also be templates of contracts or spreadsheets that you can edit rather than having to start from scratch, so do your research and/or ask (perhaps the firm has an intranet site or an internal support team that can give you a steer).

Intended recipient

Make sure that you always consider the intended recipient of your work. If it's for a client, then ensure it is short, concise and to the point (unless you are told otherwise) and that the language is not too technical or full of jargon and acronyms. If the work is for a member of your team, perhaps ask whether they would like you to keep a record of any sources you reference, whether they have a rough word limit in mind, and how they would like you to present the work (e.g. whether they would like a printed and/or an electronic copy). These are not stupid questions. In fact, they can demonstrate initiative, plus you'll be surprised at how specific some supervisors' preferences are in terms of printing and stapling!

Receiving instructions

Whenever you meet with someone, *always* bring along a pad and pen so that you are ready to write down instructions if they set you a new piece of work (or in case they give you useful guidance or insights about the firm). Once you have received instructions, you could start by summarising them back to your supervisor to check that you have understood them correctly. Ask questions if you are unclear on a particular instruction, but listen carefully: asking the same question twice will waste your supervisor's time and reflect negatively on you. If any issues arise once you have started the work, make some effort to figure out as much as possible by yourself through research. Failing this, rather than repeatedly interrupting your supervisor with questions (which can be frustrating and disruptive for them), consider listing out the questions that arise overtime and then asking them all at once when your supervisor has a free moment.

Also, don't forget to confirm the deadline. Without a deadline, it will be difficult to prioritise tasks effectively if you have more than one task on the go. You will also not know whether you have capacity to take on *further* tasks. I have been given tasks with 30 minute deadlines and others with a deadline of 7-10 days, so it's always best to ask. There might even be flexibility around your deadlines, so there's no harm in clarifying. Communication is key. It's better to ask about flexibility rather than miss a deadline (and of course, *offer* to work late or over the weekend if this is the only way you'll be able to get everything completed on time).

Work diary

Consider keeping a work diary as you go along. This will help you to remember what you've been up to if you're later asked by your supervisor (or in a final interview) to reflect upon your experiences. However, do not forget about confidentiality. If you include confidential information in your work diary, then perhaps don't take it outside the office and don't keep hold of it after the internship. Alternatively, you could avoid noting down confidential information (e.g. client names and specific details about the matters) and instead include just enough information to jog your memory about the clients, tasks and any challenges you faced. On a similar note, when making a job application after completing an internship, never include confidential details of work completed elsewhere. This could call into question your ability to adhere to the required standards of confidentiality.

Team presentations

Internships typically include a team-based exercise to test the way in which candidates interact with others on a mutual task. This could involve researching and delivering a group presentation relating to the firm in general or a particular departmen' ...may be structured as a pitch to a fictional client that focuses on the firm's capabilities, its past experience, the challenges it ...he locations in which new offices should be opened, or even the way in which it can offer greater value for money / could involve some kind of creative task or mock negotiation. If you've been tasked with preparing a pitch or group, check whether there will be a question and answer session at the end. If there will, then make sure yo' work and research inside out. You may be allowed to defer an answer to a colleague, but may also be expecte on your colleagues' work. If you are clearly familiar with one other's input, this will indicate to your assess effectively as a team. You may also want to consider supplementing a presentation with a hando presentation and make your group stand out, whilst also demonstrating creativity, effective tear organisational skills. However, perhaps distribute any handouts *after* the presentation, as the c those in the room from what you are saying *during* the presentation.

Professionalism

It should go without saying, but strive to be professional and reliable throughout the entire internship, regardless of the context. This includes being punctual, especially after social events that end late! Check the dress code before you arrive and remain smart and presentable throughout (even if some of the employees take a more casual approach). This does not necessarily mean that you must ignore casual Fridays for instance, but don't show up in shorts and flip-flops simply because you have seen a Partner or Director do so. On that note, remember you are making an impression on the *entire* firm. I was once referred to by a friend's supervisor as his "scruffy mate" after letting my appearance slip following a particularly gruelling weekend shift during my training contract. People notice, and it can be hard to restore your personal brand once it has been damaged. In addition, don't be too informal or act too casually, as this could suggest you don't care, or worse, be mistaken for arrogance. Treat everyone with courtesy and respect, whether they are your supervisor, a receptionist, an intern, a secretary, the most senior employee at the firm or one of the cleaners. It's common decency, plus you never know who will be asked for their opinion of you during or after the internship.

I have experienced interns talking negatively about other interns, without realising that one of those present happened to be a good friend of the interns under fire. Any animosity caused in this way can typically be perceived by graduate recruiters, which in my experience has not done any favours for those at fault. Also, your fellow interns may well be your future colleagues, so treat them with respect in order to get your working relationship off on the right foot. I have also overheard interns talking negatively about other firms to graduate recruiters, presumably in an attempt to demonstrate that the current firm is their preference. However, bad mouthing other firms could convey a degree of arrogance and suggest that you lack professionalism. Moreover, graduate recruiters tend to move between firms fairly frequently, so could end up subsequently joining the firm you were badmouthing (if you have interned at that other firm, this switch might even happen before that firm has made their final decision about whether to offer you a job!). Two of the graduate recruiters running the final internship that I undertook had previously worked at other firms when I had attended open days and internships at those other firms. One had even co-ordinated my interview day at a different firm only a few months earlier! Moral of the story? Be very careful about what you say to other interns, graduate recruiters and employees of firms more generally.

Final Interviews

Internships typically involve some sort of final interview towards the end. For some firms, this interview is as important as any other element of the assessment (if not more important), whereas other firms might treat it more as a casual debrief. Either way, by the time this interview comes around, your motivation for wanting to join the firm should be fully formed and well-articulated. Whilst three or four structured reasons for wanting to work for a particular firm may scrape you through an interview before an internship, much more may be expected of you in an end-of-internship interview. Having spent a number of weeks immersed in a firm's culture, meeting various employees and engaging in real work, your reasons for wanting to work at the firm will have to be more personal, more substantive and less derivative of the firm's marketing materials.

Ask yourself how your impression of the firm evolved throughout the internship. Were any of your preconceptions confirmed or dispelled? Were there people you particularly enjoyed meeting? If so, what was it about those people? Does the culture really resonate with you? If so, describe the culture and why it appeals. Have you seen first-hand how the firm's values permeate throughout the office? If so, be prepared to discuss the meaning of these values and give examples of how they were upheld in practice. Did you learn more about the training on offer and if so, did this help to differentiate the firm from its competitors? What challenges did you face? Were there pieces of work that you found particularly interesting or engaging? Be prepared to discuss the work you completed in detail, including what you enjoyed about it and how it fit into the wider context of the relevant matters.

Also prepare some carefully considered questions for your interviewers. These might relate to your interviewer's career and motivations, or the firm's culture, its future strategies, the challenges it is facing (or may face in the future), its training or anything else you can think of that demonstrates your genuine interest in working there. If you do plan on asking about the firm's challenges and future strategies, make sure you have carried out some related research, as you may well be asked to express a personal opinion. Also be prepared to give feedback. What have you enjoyed? What did you not enjoy so much? How could the internship be improved? How does the firm compare to other firms you have interned at? Has your opinion of the firm changed since your internship commenced? Did the internship match up to your prior expectations and preconceptions? Obviously don't give scathing feedback, but try to think of something constructive. For example, would you have liked to have heard more about what a broader range of the firm's practice areas do? Or had the opportunity to learn about business processes such as business development?